RED
HOT
HANDOUTS!

Taking the HO HUM
out of Handouts

Dave Arch
Introduction by Bob Pike

JOSSEY-BASS/PFEIFFER
A Wiley Company
www.pfeiffer.com

Creative Training Techniques
Press

Published by

JOSSEY-BASS/PFEIFFER

A Wiley Company
989 Market Street
San Francisco, CA 94103-1741
415.433.1740; Fax 415.433.0499
800.274.4434; Fax 800.569.0443

www.pfeiffer.com

OTHER PRODUCTS BY THE AUTHOR

Techniques And Tricks for Trainers (two day seminar)

Tricks For Trainers, Volume I

Tricks For Trainers, Volume II

The Tricks For Trainers Video Library (3 volumes)

First Impressions/Lasting Impressions

Showmanship For Presenters

Trainer Bingo

THANK YOU!
To Sandi Dufault, Rebecca Tolle, and Candace Hiatt. This book stands as continuing evidence of your wonderful abilities for taking hazy handout concepts and giving them clarity as you tirelessly transformed them time and time again into handout graphics that will now be used by trainers throughout the world! You're the best!

TABLE OF CONTENTS

INTRODUCTION BY BOB PIKE, C.S.P. i

HOW TO USE THIS BOOK (Please read this first) iii

HANDOUT TEMPLATES 1

In the following 24 different Handout Tmplates, you're sure to find many that will fit your training content! Then just copy the template — adding your content!

A BETTER LETTER. 3

A MAZING! 7

PAPER PUZZLER 11

SCULPTURE 15

TRY YOUR LUCK! 19

LIGHT ART 25

RECESS REVIEW 29

SQUARED! 33

PUZZLE PIECES 37

A LETTER FROM HOME I 41

A LETTER FROM HOME II 45

HOP TO IT! 49

AIRBORNE 55

AERODYNAMIC 59

ON YOUR MARK! 63

INSTANT SEPARATION 67

COIN TOSS 71

A STAR IS BORN. 75

CAPTURE THE CONTENT! 79

HOLDING WATER 83

PRIZES! 87

PRIZES! PRIZES! 91

ACTION GRAPHICS 95

This section contains 26 Action Graphics for adding energy to any handout — increasing participants' interaction and retention!

FLYING HIGH. 97

THE WRITING ON THE WALL 99

VANISHING ART. 101

COME IN! 103

TRIANGULAR! 105

TIC-TAC-TOE TOP SECRET 107

FINGER PLAY 109

A HOME RUN 111

AN EYE OPENER 113

CENTERED 115

TIGHTROPE WALK 117

PENDULUM PAPER 119

EMPLOYMENT TEST 121

THE IMPOSSIBLE HOLE. 123

THE TRICK THAT FOOLED EINSTEIN 125

FINGER TALK 127

ALPHABET SOUP 129

WHEELING 131

RIGHTSIDE UP! 133

MAGIC SQUARES 135

PITCHFORKED 139

HANDOUT HINTS 141

25 different proven ideas — bringing NEW life to any handout!

X-RAY TUBE 143

STRIKE UP THE BAND 145

PAPER AND COIN DROP 147

HANDOUT GRAB 149

HANDOUT PICKUP 151

MYSTERY ASHES 153

THE CANDLE/PART 1 155

THE CANDLE/PART 2 157

STICK PUSH 159

TEARING UP 161

TUBULAR. 163

TRAINING TRANSPOSITION 165

THE HANDOUT BOOMERANG . . . 167

SAMSON 169

PAPER BRIDGE 171

RAINDROPS 173

TELEPATHETIC. 175

ORIGAMIED 177

SPEEDY SCISSORS SNIP! 179

FINGERTIP BALANCING 181

PAPER DOLLS 183

FOOT LIFT 185

THROUGH THE EYE OF A NEEDLE . . . 187

ZIP I & II!. 189

THE THORNLESS ROSE 191

INTRODUCTION BY BOB PIKE, C.S.P.

In many seminars I've said that preparation is 80 percent of being creative in any presentation. That preparation includes how you put together a handout. For many trainers a handout is an afterthought — instead it should be a forethought.

A handout becomes a valuable resource both during the training and after — but only when it's planned that way. Some trainers follow the school of thought that says "Minimize handouts, they only distract." Others give the handout after a presentation. What we teach in Creative Training Techniques and what Dave Arch models in *Red Hot Handouts* is that the handout is an integral part of the training. It becomes a valuable tool to involve participants during the training program — and to keep them coming back to it as a resource long after the program.

Use this book as a reference. You don't need to use everything in each presentation you design, but rather use the various unique handout designs to add spice, involvement, and memory value to your presentation.

The handouts that are presented and modeled here are designed not for you to use as is, but to modify, adjust, adapt — and then adopt. As always, you are the expert when it comes to understanding your audience and subject matter. Regardless of the audience, however, you'll find material in this book to help increase the impact of your presentation — and to make that presentation more memorable.

Too many trainers and presenters make the mistake of thinking that you can have fun or content. It's time to change that thinking to having fun WITH content. Every handout enables you to make a powerful learning point — often faster than traditional methods might allow. At the same time the memory value is increased so that participants can retain more readily and apply the content more easily when they return to their jobs.

Go through each handout model that Dave presents. As you look at it ask yourself two questions:

1. How and where can I modify, adjust, or adapt this to my own content?; and,

2. What is the risk factor to my group?

My suggestion would be to use a *Red Hot Handout* design no more than once per hour in a presentation. Use it to change the pace, emphasize a key point, etc. Overuse, however, regardless of the large variety, starts to make the handout or associated activity the focus, rather than the content.

As you begin to use these in your presentations try designing one new handout to add to a present course. Use one that you think of as being "sure fire." As you see the results it will increase your confidence in adding activities and handouts that you might consider to be higher risk, but now the risk factor is reduced because your confidence level is increased.

So let me turn you over now to my associate, Dave Arch, and enjoy your exploration of *Red Hot Handouts.*

HOW TO USE THIS BOOK

For too long presenters have relegated the handout to the lowly position of being the very last presentational component given any consideration. This unique book could change all that!

Within its covers you'll discover 75 different ideas for making your next handout an integral part of your presentational strategy. This book's ideas have been divided into three sections.

Section One contains 24 templates that can be copied onto the back of your handout. Some of these uniquely combine origami with handouts. At the conclusion of your session, your participants can turn their handouts over, follow the instructions on the pattern and create a content-related paper sculpture! Others help transform your handout into a closing activity or review tool.

Section Two presents 26 unique graphics that can be used to make your handouts more interactive. Optical illusions, simple magic tricks, and puzzles give these Action Graphics energy for increasing participants' content retention and training transfer.

Section Three explains 25 interactive activities for use with any handout! Without changing your current handouts at all, add one or two of these activities for creating greater focus in your next session.

May this book make your handouts an increasingly indispensable component in your training toolbox!

HANDOUT TEMPLATES

In the following 24 different handout templates, you're sure to find many that will fit your training! Then just copy the template — adding your content!

A BETTER LETTER

By copying this template onto the back of your handout, any handout makes itself into its own envelope with only a few folds. Training transfer made easier through follow-up applicational and accountability mailings after the session is over!

A MAZING!

This maze looks like it would take no time at all to solve; but it requires more than first thought! It customizes easily to your content and your trainees will soon understand that persistence has its own reward!

PAPER PUZZLER

Imagine a paper puzzle with content messages hidden deep inside its folds! Finding the messages is a puzzling challenge! However, better than that is the fact that your participants will keep this handout to show others while reviewing your content at the same time!

SCULPTURE

The culmination of this handout's use is watching it transform into a very unusual sculpture! The final product always intrigues and makes a wonderful display of your main emphases!

TRY YOUR LUCK!

Using a famous carnival game as your handout, your presentation will not soon be forgotten as your participants try their luck throughout the presentation and are then left with a tangible reminder of your content!

LIGHT ART

Here are three patterns for designing very interactive handouts that change dramatically when held up to light!

RECESS REVIEW

This unique origami handout has great content applications and then makes a fun review tool for up to EIGHT content areas.

SQUARED!

This handout comes as puzzle pieces designed to make a square. Putting it all together will take some teamwork!

PUZZLE PIECES

Can you make the letter "F" with just these five handout pieces? It will take your entire table team to make it happen!

A LETTER FROM HOME I

This letter enables the trainer to use the handout to mysteriously introduce or review up to TWELVE different content emphases in an interactive manner.

A LETTER FROM HOME II

This letter guides the group through an unbelievable experience of reviewing up to EIGHT different content emphases.

HOP TO IT!

"Let's hop to it!" is really illustrated by this simple origami fold that's fun and easy to teach! By simply following the instructions on the back of the handout, each person finishes with a giant paper frog that really jumps!

AIRBORNE

Do you have trouble with your trainees returning evaluations? Not anymore! Duplicate these lines onto the back of your evaluations and your participants can fly them to the front of the room! Each handout becomes a paper airplane! An additional idea for training transfer is also included with this template.

AERODYNAMIC

Turn any handout into an old airplane with wings that really flap! "Any idea can carry you somewhere!" is the slogan proudly painted on the airplane's side. This is excellent for reminding every participant how we can always build on even the silliest ideas!

ON YOUR MARK!

With a few folds, this handout becomes a race's starter pistol! When everyone fires their guns, a special content summary message appears at the end of each gun barrel!

INSTANT SEPARATION

This handout works best when covering positive and negative aspects of any subject. Sixteen different areas can be emphasized. Then when each person folds their handout into sixteenths, cuts around all four edges of the packet (through all thicknesses of the paper), and deals the resultant faceup pieces into one pile and the face down pieces into another; the positive qualities will be in one pile and negative qualities in the other! It's unbelievable to see the separation work!

COIN TOSS

This handout becomes an instant carnival game for great review! It's an excellent energizer for team play!

A STAR IS BORN

The trainer folds his or her handout and with one snip of the scissors, transforms it into a perfectly formed star. It's a great closer for any training session.

CAPTURE THE CONTENT!

Watch your outline become a reinforcing game at the conclusion of your session.

HOLDING WATER

Do your content ideas hold water? Good question! However when your participants finish folding your handout, they will have a paper cup that can actually hold water!

PRIZES!

Print this number grid and prize listing on the back of your handout and then use it to review content. Each person circles different numbers in the grid to select one of the prizes...and amazingly enough although everyone selects different numbers, they lead everyone to winning the SAME PRIZE! The trainer controls which prize everyone wins! A great activity to use just before break!

PRIZES! PRIZES!

Still another way to work the previous review and prize giveaway to bring even greater variety into your training session!

ACTION GRAPHICS

This section contains 26 graphics for adding action to any handout — increasing participant interaction and retention!

FLYING HIGH

Watch the airplane in this artwork slowly turn right before your eyes. Great for emphasizing change. Just copy it onto your handout and watch the fun!

THE WRITING ON THE WALL

You can make your trainees see your summarizing message floating in the air around the room. Here's how! Works excellent with any content!

VANISHING ART

Here's how to make any handout graphic vanish right before each of your trainee's eyes! Many applications!

COME IN!

Use this one on your next handout and watch your participants really come alive! A bird and a cage are seen in a picture right next to each other. Yet as the group follows your instructions, they watch the bird slowly walk into the cage! Use your imagination to customize this to your content with any two pictures of your choice dramatically coming together! Two additional graphics included for differing applications.

TRIANGULAR!

How many triangles can your trainees find in this piece of modern art? There are always more than anyone first suspects! That's how it is with most learning too! There's more to any subject than anyone first anticipates!

TIC-TAC-TOE TOP SECRET

Decorate your handout with this tic-tac-toe border and demonstrate how important having a system is to winning anything! Imagine never losing at tic-tac-toe even though you play blindfolded — never seeing where the other person places their mark! That's exactly what you do as you illustrate how many things become possible once a system has been mastered!

FINGER PLAY

In this artwork, the participants bring the graphic to life as their fingers become ears! It's a riot!

A HOME RUN

Watch the baseball slowly move in a home run arch right into the glove! A golf ball graphic magically dropping into the hole is also included.

AN EYE OPENER

The lady in this graphic slowly and mysteriously opens her eyes as you watch her!

CENTERED

Is the dot in the middle of this triangle? You'll never know for sure without measuring! Content can surround the triangle on this handout!

TIGHTROPE WALK

This poor tightrope walker's rope has broken! Watch it magically come together right before your eyes! Two other versions included for differing applications!

PENDULUM PAPER

The chart on the handout brings each pendulum to life as the trainer asks specific questions — causing the individual pendulums to move in response! It's spooky!

EMPLOYMENT TEST

Through a cute story and this artwork, the trainer explains how the company's luckiest job applicant got hired! Of course, the real name of that employee will always remain a secret!

THE IMPOSSIBLE HOLE

What's that hole doing in the handout? A dime size hole in the handout looks too small to have a quarter go through it…but it's not! Many things only *look* impossible!

THE TRICK THAT FOOLED EINSTEIN

This magic trick actually fooled the great scientist, Albert Einstein! A prediction is printed on the handout and seen by all ahead of time. A handful of small content-oriented items (possibly coins) is grabbed from a pile by a volunteer from the audience. When the prediction is read, it foretells exactly the number of items the volunteer selected. It can then be repeated with a different prediction and a different result. Great for starting a group talking about possible solutions to this trick! Gets them truly involved in a problem-solving frame of mind.

FINGER TALK

Everyone experiences this one together as the trainer asks them to each move one finger or another in response to a series of lesson questions. Imagine their surprise when they all find themselves unable to move one of their fingers even though they all want to!

ALPHABET SOUP

This teaches you how to customize a classic observation test to your own content! Applicable to any content!

WHEELING

This stationary circular design suddenly begins to rotate just like a wheel!

RIGHTSIDE UP!

Turn this graphic upside down and you won't believe the sudden change!

MAGIC SQUARES

Using a two-digit number randomly suggested by your participants at the beginning of your training session, progressively build this action graphic until you finish the session with a matrix of sixteen numbers that add together horizontally, vertically, diagonally and over twenty different directions to total the number first suggested by the group. Your trainees will be amazed, and you will have shown how amazing accomplishments can be when one is willing to take the time to design and follow a system.

PITCHFORKED

How many prongs on this weird looking pitchfork? Better count again! Our own beliefs change!

HANDOUT HINTS

27 different proven ideas — bringing NEW life to any handout!

X-RAY TUBE

Sci-fi fans take note! Any handout becomes an x-ray tube. It will look exactly as though you can peer through your own hand when you use this tube!

STRIKE UP THE BAND

Any handout can be simply transformed into a flute that really plays! You and your participants will be making beautiful music in no time!

PAPER AND COIN DROP

The challenge is to drop a coin and a small piece of handout paper at the same time — having the paper reach the floor first. It can be done!

HANDOUT GRAB

The nervous system really gets a workout as a volunteer participant tries for a prize!

HANDOUT PICKUP

Although the handout is right in front of him, the volunteer can't get it! The feeling of helplessness is often a good feeling to experience.

MYSTERY ASHES

Baring his forearm, the trainer shows that it's clean. Yet when the handout is burned and the ashes applied to the arm, a word summarizing the lesson slowly begins to materialize right on his skin! It's weird and memorable!

THE CANDLE/PART 1

Anyone can blow out a candle! Sure! It's easy! However, no one will believe how difficult it is when blowing through a funnel-shaped handout! Everything is difficult with the wrong tool!

THE CANDLE/PART 2

Now nonchalantly pick up the candle you just used in the previous demonstration and eat it! Your participants will definitely sit up and pay attention after that!

STICK PUSH

As the handout lays on the floor, three participants attempt to push the broomstick down onto it. With one hand behind his/her back, the trainer successfully resists their attempts. It's a wonderful example of working smarter not harder!

TEARING UP

Can you believe that tearing a handout into three pieces could be so difficult! But it is!

TUBULAR

Take a few moments before the session and you can turn any handout into a magician's production tube. Roll the handout into a tube and produce dollar bills (or other content-related items) as though by magic!

TRAINING TRANSPOSITION

With this variation of an old carnival game, you'll use three pieces of paper as your handout — teaching your participants how to roll them in such a way that they trade places even when another person's finger is holding them down!

THE HANDOUT BOOMERANG

The trainer promises to throw the session handout as hard as possible. She promises that the handout will stop in mid-air (without hitting anything or anyone) and return to her hand! And it does!

SAMSON

Use some of this special paper to make a duplicate handout and have some fun!

PAPER BRIDGE

Can you form your handout into a bridge between two glasses so that it can support a third glass of water? This energizer gets everyone involved!

RAINDROPS

The ear is fooled as an imaginary ceiling leak begins to produce audible sounds of dripping right onto the handout! The power of suggestion is very powerful!

TELEPATHETIC!

After anyone writes on a handout, the trainer is able to tell exactly what's on it!

ORIGAMIED

There's a prize waiting for anyone who can fold the handout in half more than seven times! No one will be able (no matter what size the paper might be), but the group will be energized trying!

SPEEDY SCISSORS SNIP!

With quite a flair, the trainer tosses the handout into the air and apparently uses his scissors to snip a piece off the handout in mid-air! It's showy! It's easy! Everyone enjoys learning it!

FINGERTIP BALANCING

With a drum roll from the group, the trainer balances the entire handout from just one corner on his fingertip! Everyone wants to try once they see how it's done!

PAPER DOLLS

With a few snips of her scissors, the trainer folds the handout and cuts out a perfect line of content icons (a.k.a. paper dolls) as a wonderful way to close the training session!

FOOT LIFT

Standing with his or her right foot against the wall, a volunteer attempts to lift his or her left foot into the air balancing the handout on the top of his or her shoe! The difficulty is hilarious! Finally, the trainer shows that it can be done!

THROUGH THE EYE OF A NEEDLE

Pin one of these impossibilities to each handout and listen to the discussion begin! This sewing needle has at least twenty seven threads through the single eye! How is it even possible? The trainer isn't telling!

ZIP I & II!

Can you remove the handout so that the stack of quarters remain on the opening of the ketchup bottle? Remember hearing about the tablecloth and dishes trick? Give it a try! Then increase the difficulty and try to think of an entirely new way!

THE THORNLESS ROSE

With a wonderful story about a rose and the power of one person being willing to change, the trainer summarizes the training session in a very powerful manner while slowly transforming his or her own handout into an intriguing paper rose.

HANDOUT TEMPLATES

In the following 24 different handout templates, you're sure to find many that will fit your training! Then just copy the template — adding your content! It's that easy!

The templates in this section were designed to be reproduced for use in your own presentations. To photocopy, simply align the upper right hand corner of the template page with the upper right corner guide on the copier.

A Better Letter

By copying this template onto the back of your handout, any handout makes itself into its own envelope with only a few folds. Training transfer made easier through follow-up applicational and accountability mailings after the session is over!

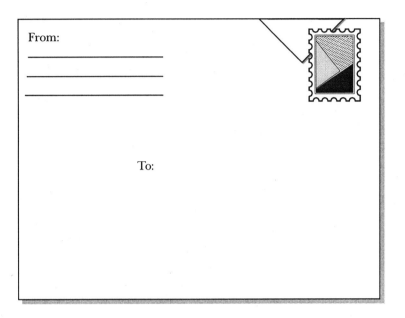

Directions

At the conclusion of your training, give each participant a copy of the following template. Have them address the template to themselves and write a letter to themselves (on the blank side) with their thoughts about how they'd like to apply the content just learned.

After they have completed the letter and folded their envelope, collect the envelopes and mail them back to each participant in thirty to sixty days as a reminder of their applicational goals.

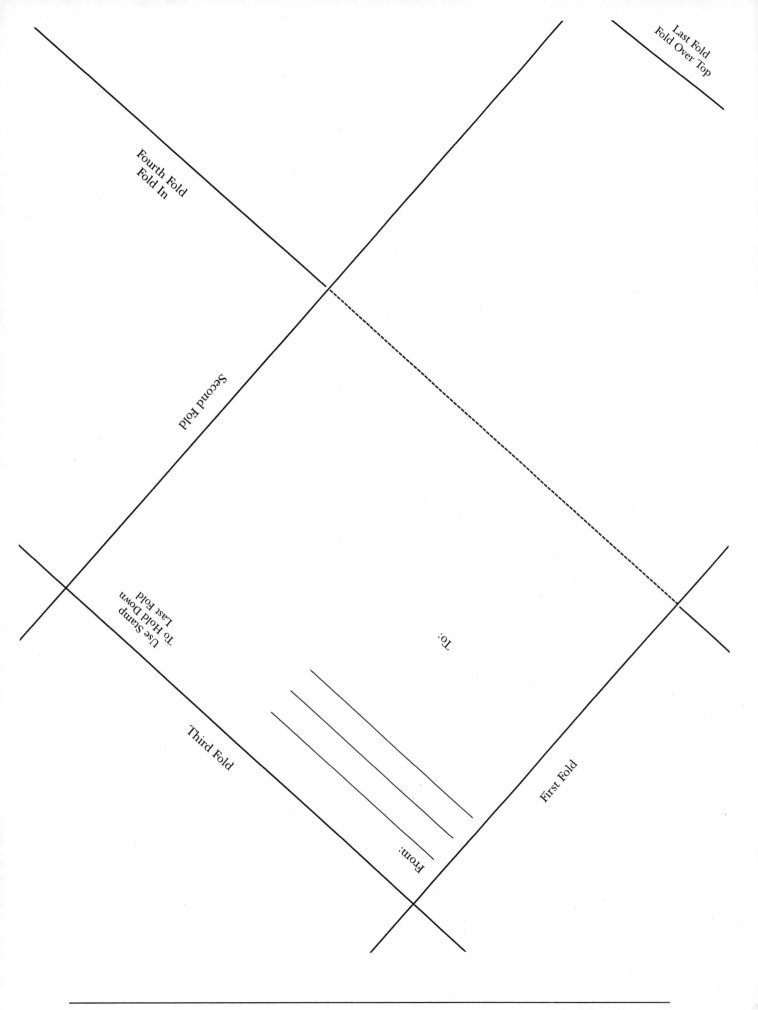

Last Fold
Fold Over Top

Fourth Fold
Fold In

Second Fold

Use Stamp
To Hold Down
Last Fold

Second Fold
Last Fold

To:

Third Fold

First Fold

From:

A MAZING!

This maze template looks like it would take no time at all to solve, but it requires more than first thought! The center customizes easily with an icon pertaining to your content, and your trainees will soon understand that persistence has its own reward!

A Mazing Solution

Start Here

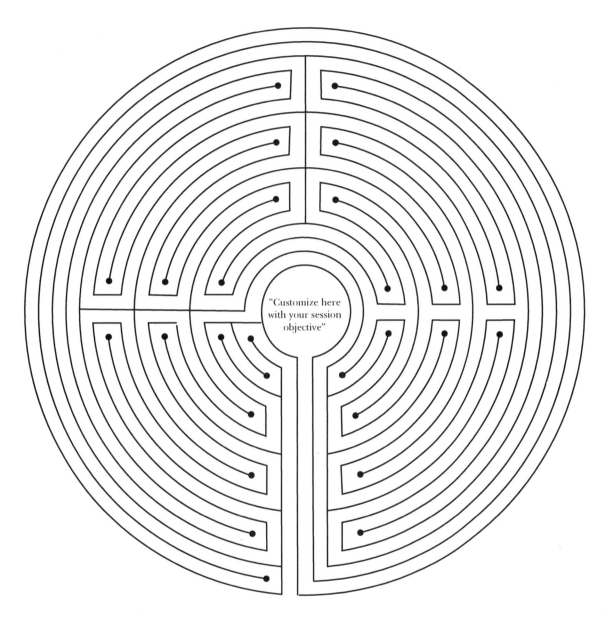

"Customize here with your session objective"

Start Here

PAPER PUZZLER

Imagine a paper puzzle with content messages hidden deep inside its folds! Finding the messages is a puzzling challenge! However, better than that is the fact that your participants will keep this handout to show others while reviewing your content at the same time!

Square in the middle

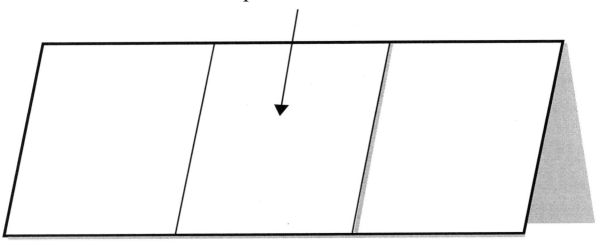

Directions

1. Taking a copy of the following template, widthwise fold the paper into half and then in half again so that the paper is evenly divided into four sections.

    Then cutting on the dotted lines only, cut out a flap from the middle of the paper — leaving one edge of the flap attached to the paper as in the diagram.

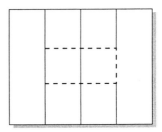

2. Laying the paper on the table in front of you as in the diagram, fold the far left panel over on top of the panel to its right.

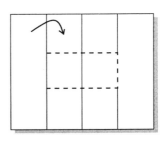

3. Pull the flap completely under the paper so that it sticks out from under the left edge of the paper.

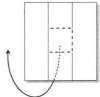

4. Fold this entire flap up over the top of the paper so that the flap now lies on top of the packet.

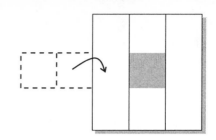

5. Holding the flap down so that it doesn't fold back, fold the two right-hand panels over the packet to the left.

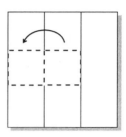

6. Now fold the left hand panel over the top of the right-hand panel.

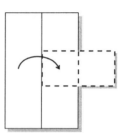

7. Then fold the flap piece over the top of the left-hand piece so that it lays on top of the packet.

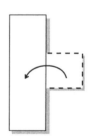

8. Finally, take a piece of clear tape and tape the flap to the first single piece of paper directly under it. Be sure to tape the flap to only the single piece of paper!

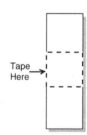

Now...open the assembled paper puzzle like a book (from left to right) — folding that front cover clear around to the underside of the packet. You are now looking at the front of the paper puzzle. By repeating this same series of openings to the paper puzzle and bending it back on its spines, you'll be able to open THE SPINES to discover completely new inside surfaces. You'll actually have three different internal surfaces. Hide your secret summary message on the innermost surface and your trainees will have great fun trying to find it!

As still yet another idea, the Paper Puzzler makes a very unique table tent for displaying participants' names at the training table.

The following template will show you where to put content messages for maximum impact.

No
Tearing
Needed!

No
Ripping
Necessary!

Don't
Give Up!

Keep
Looking!

Your Message
Goes Here

Your Message
Goes Here

Your Message
Goes Here

Your Message
Goes Here

Your Message
Goes Here

SCULPTURE

The culmination of this handout's use is watching it transform into a very unusual sculpture! The final product always intrigues and makes a wonderful display of your main emphases!

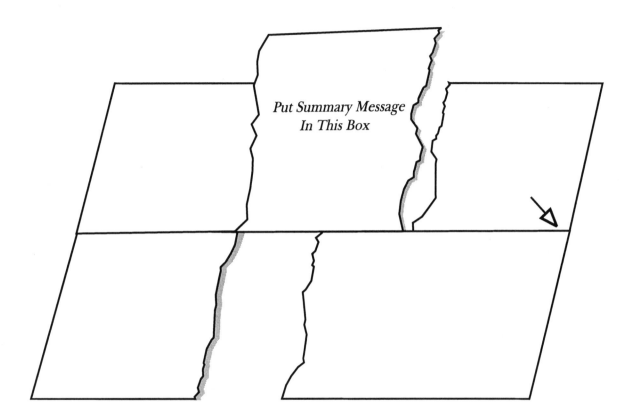

Put Summary Message In This Box

Copy the following templates onto the front and back of your handout. Your main emphases can then be written in boxes #1-4. If you also then print a summary message in the designated square, the finished sculpture will display your four points with a summarizing statement standing up from the sculpture billboard fashion.

Directions

(A) Fold both ways on solid line and open out flat again.

(B) Tear along all dotted lines.

(C) Put arrow between index finger and thumb of right hand-twisting down and away from you at the same time.

Put Summary Message In This Box Between Dotted Lines

2

1

3

Put Summary Message
In This Box
Between Dotted
Lines

4

TRY YOUR LUCK!

Using a famous carnival game as your handout, your presentation will not soon be forgotten as your participants try their luck throughout the presentation and are then left with a tangible reminder of your content!

Directions

You might consider filling in the larger circle template with a word(s) denoting the negative aspect of your training topic (i.e., for Customer Service the larger circle might read "Customer Dissatisfaction," for Time Management it might read "Time Waste," etc.).

Then have the five smaller circles filled in with those steps that help control the negative aspect of your training topic which you printed on the large circle.

The five smaller circles must be dropped one at a time from a height of at least six inches onto the big circle. The winner must completely cover the large circle with NONE of the large circle (negative content aspect) showing through!

Most will attempt to drop them like the **Pattern A** below. **Pattern B** is a more efficient way to get the job done. However, it won't happen without practice!

Pattern A

Pattern B

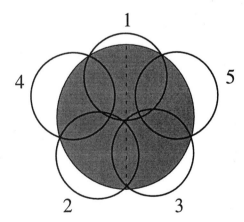

LIGHT ART

Here are three patterns for designing very interactive handouts that change dramatically when held up to the light!

Directions

Hold any of the artwork up to the light and watch the change in the picture! Just copy one of them onto the front and back of your next handout and watch the fun begin.

The author has found that printing this artwork on the front and back of a turquoise paper (such as Kinko's 20# Lunar Blue) yields the best result.

QUALITY

RECESS REVIEW

This unique origami handout has great content applications and then makes a fun review tool for up to EIGHT content areas.

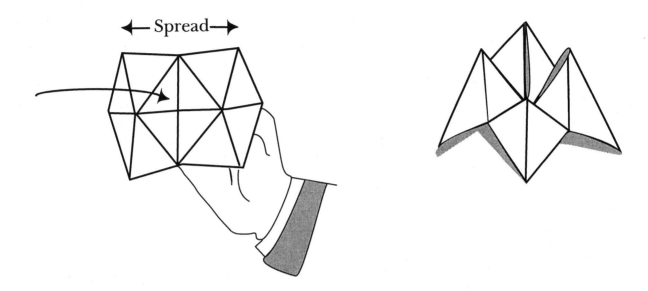

← Spread →

Directions

Although at first glance this might appear to be one of the more complicated of the templates, it actually is one of the most enjoyable when teaching a series of up to eight emphases that require review for maximum retention.

As you look at the template you will notice on one side a series of spokes as on a wheel with numbers printed close to the hub of those spokes. Participants will write your key emphases between the spokes beginning with the number one section of the spokes and continuing through to the number eight section (as formed by the spokes).

You will also notice a corresponding set of numbers around the outside of the square handout. This is where you will print a review question that corresponds to the point you will be making in that particular numbered spoke. In other words, as close to the number 1 question mark as possible, you will print a review question that corresponds to the point you'll be making (and having your participants write) in the number 1 section of the spokes.

Make sure that you orient the letters in your question to correspond to the orientation of the question mark.

At the conclusion of your presentation, you will have them turn the handout facedown and fold the four corners into the center. Then they will turn the handout face up again and fold the new corners into the center. If you now hold the handout as in the picture above you will notice that your review questions cover the answers as written by the participants between the spokes.

Have them work with a partner selecting one of the numbers — trying to answer the question as printed on the handout. The partner then peels back that section to see if they are correct. Then it's the other partner's turn to try their hand at it. However, they are not allowed to select the question whose answer they just saw (since two answers will always be exposed when the question flap is pulled back).

Have each person continue this process with a partner until all eight emphases have been reviewed. It's fun! For many it will also bring back memories of school when this device was used as a game on the playground.

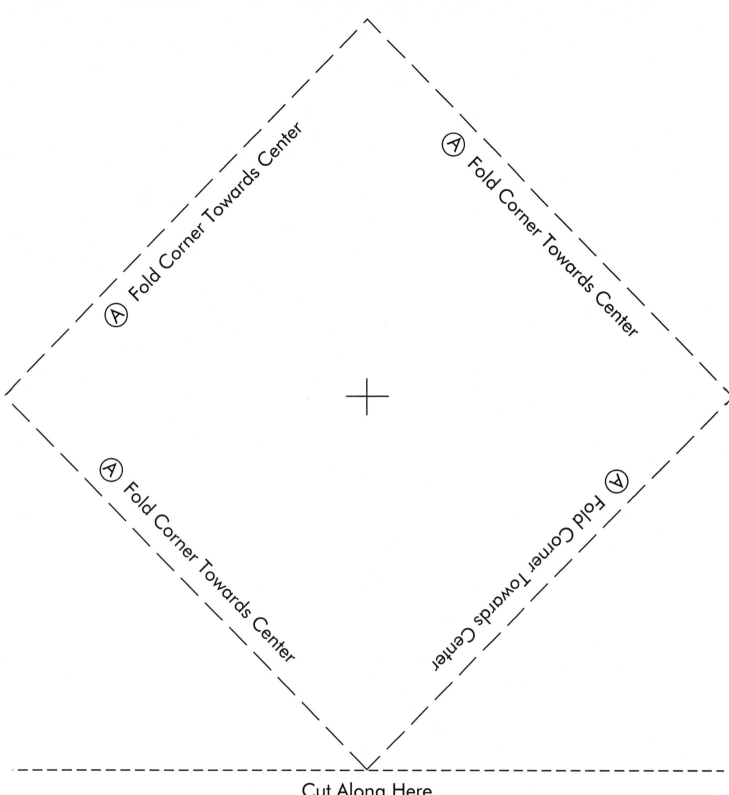

Fold Corner Towards Center

Ⓐ Fold Corner Towards Center

Ⓐ Fold Corner Towards Center

Ⓐ Fold Corner Towards Center

Ⓐ Fold Corner Towards Center

Cut Along Here

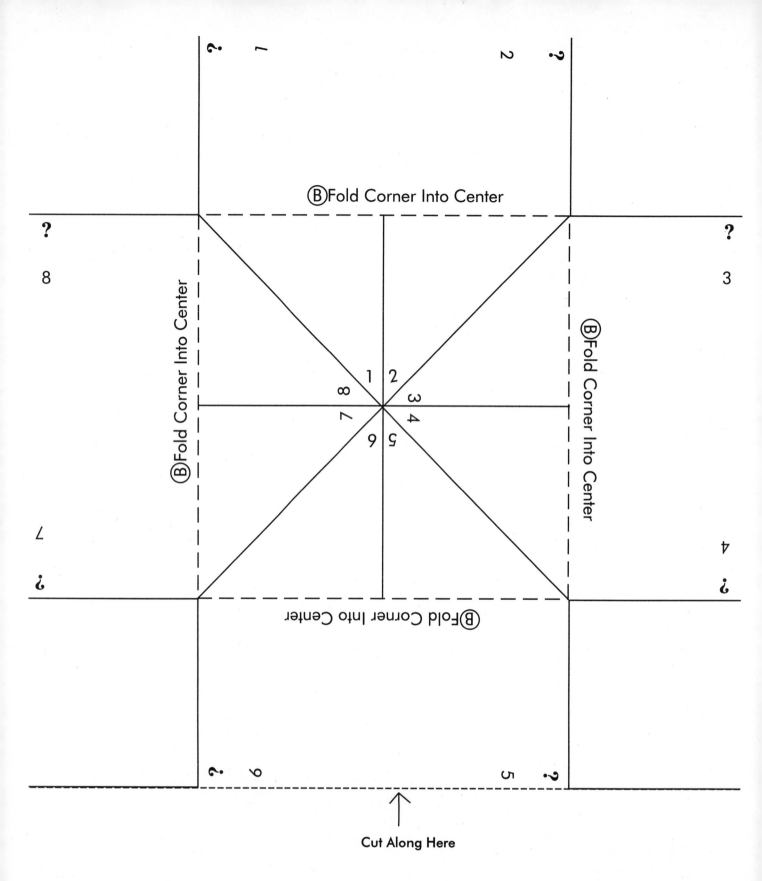

SQUARED!

This handout comes as puzzle pieces designed to make a square. Putting it all together will take some teamwork!

Squared! Solution

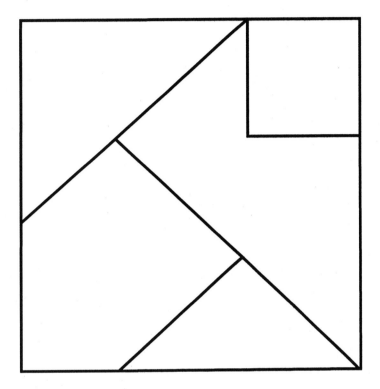

Directions

After having them write content emphasis in each of the five pieces on the following template, have them cut out and give a prize to the first group who can put the pieces together to form a square. It takes teamwork to effectively apply most content!

PUZZLE PIECES

Can you make the letter "F" with just these five handout pieces? It will take your entire table team to make it happen.

Puzzle Pieces Solution

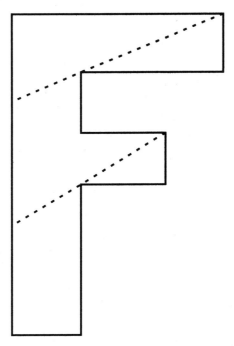

Directions

Use the following template to make your handout. Then have your participants write a different content component from your training in each of the five pieces.

At the conclusion of your training, have your participants cut out the pieces and attempt to assemble the pieces into the letter "F" — having a prize for the first person (or table team) to successfully complete the assignment.

Have the letter "F" represent a summarizing word for your presentation (i.e., "friendliness" for a customer service presentation, "frugality" for a cost control program or "first" for how to remain in first place in a competitive market place.)

A Letter From Home I

This letter enables the trainer to use the handout to mysteriously introduce or review TWELVE different content emphases in an interactive manner.

Directions

In the book, *Tricks For Trainers, Volume I,* there is a review idea based upon a letter supposedly received from an uncle who believes he's psychic.

This template and the following one build on that theme.

Use the template for your handouts — filling in the boxes with twelve words that help review your own content. Prepare an overhead transparency from the completed handout. You will also need to rewrite parts of the following letter so that it appears to be a letter coming from an uncle of yours. Fill in the appropriate blank with your own content word. When ready for review, have a participant read the following letter as the other participants follow the instructions with their own handout and/or watch a volunteer carry out the letter's instructions on the overhead.

Although it seems as though there is a completely free movement around the handout, everyone will always end in the box that's in the 1:00 position!

A LETTER FROM HOME I

Dear Dave,

I will again attempt to prove to you my psychic powers! Maybe this time you'll believe!

I'm concentrating on one of the words you have before you on the overhead! Follow my instructions carefully, and I will lead you to discover the very word that's in my mind.

Before we begin, take a moment to select in the privacy of your own mind any number between one and thirty. Don't tell anyone that number! Go ahead and do that now.

Is there any way I could know that number?

You think not? Let's see!

Standing to the side of the overhead, place your finger on the coin at the top of the circle.

Now move the coin onto the word below it on the count of "one."

Move your finger COUNTERCLOCKWISE around the circle — continuing to count aloud (next being "two") on each word until you reach your mentally selected number.

Go ahead and do that now.

Now if you begin from where you are and count CLOCKWISE to your secret number, you'll be touching the word that's on my mind.

This time to make it even more fun…as you call out the number of your count, have the group call out the word your finger is touching.

Count again now!

Are you now touching my word? "MY WORD!" is what you're going to say when I tell you that I've been thinking all this time about the word _____ (fill in with your review word at the 1:00 position)!

Thank you very much for selecting the number you did!

You have helped me prove my power again!

Your friend,

Dr. Albert Shyster

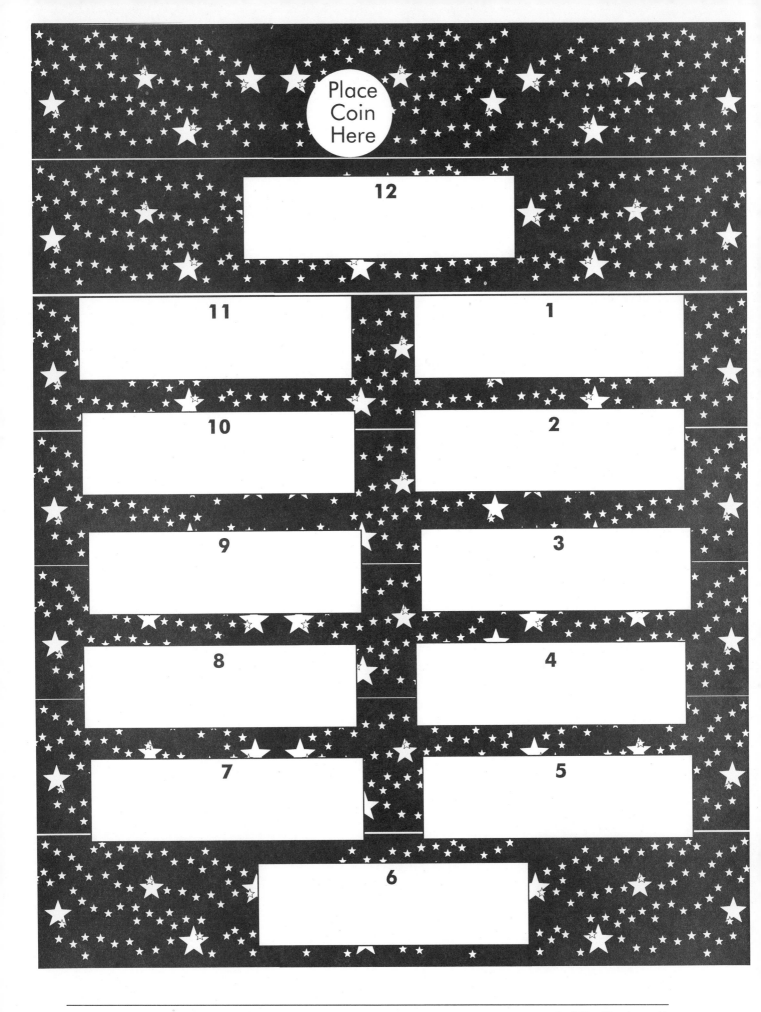

Place
Coin
Here

12

11

1

10

2

9

3

8

4

7

5

6

A LETTER FROM HOME II

This letter guides the group through an unbelievable experience of reviewing EIGHT different content emphases.

Directions

In the book, *Tricks For Trainers, Volume I,* there is a review idea based upon a letter supposedly received from an uncle who believes he's psychic.

This template and the previous one build on that theme.

Use the template for your handouts — filling in the boxes with eight words that help review your own content. Prepare an overhead transparency from the completed handout. You will also need to rewrite parts of the following letter so that it appears to be a letter coming from an uncle of yours. Fill in the appropriate blank with your own content word. When ready for review, have a participant read the following letter as the other participants follow the instructions with their own handout and/or watch a volunteer carry out the letter's instructions on the overhead.

Although it seems as though there is a completely free movement around the handout, everyone will always end in the box that's in the 1:00 position!

Note: As you might speculate after comparing this activity with the previous one, this great review technique can be adapted to fit ANY NUMBER of content review items from four through many! By using the templates as your pattern and adjusting the wording in the letter, you will have a closing for your training session that your participants will long remember…and tell others about too!

A LETTER FROM HOME II

Dear Dave,

I will again attempt to prove to you my psychic powers! Maybe this time you'll believe!

I'm concentrating on one of the words you have before you on the overhead! Follow my instructions carefully, and I will lead you to discover the very word that's in my mind.

Before we begin, take a moment to select in the privacy of your own mind, any number between one and 30. Don't tell anyone that number! Go ahead and do that now.

Is there any way I could know that number?

You think not? Let's see!

Standing to the side of the overhead, place your finger on the coin at the top of the circle.

Now move the coin onto the word below it on the count of "one."

Move your finger COUNTERCLOCKWISE around the circle — continuing to count aloud on each word until you reach your mentally selected number.

Go ahead and do that now.

Now if you begin from where you are and count CLOCKWISE to your secret number, you'll be touching the word that's on my mind.

This time to make it even more fun…as you call out the number of your count, have the group call out the word your finger is touching.

Count again now!

Are you now touching my word? "MY WORD!" is what you're going to say when I tell you that I've been thinking all this time about the word _____ (fill in with your review word at the 1:00 position)!

Thank you very much for selecting the number you did!

You have helped me prove my power again!

Your friend,

Dr. Albert Shyster

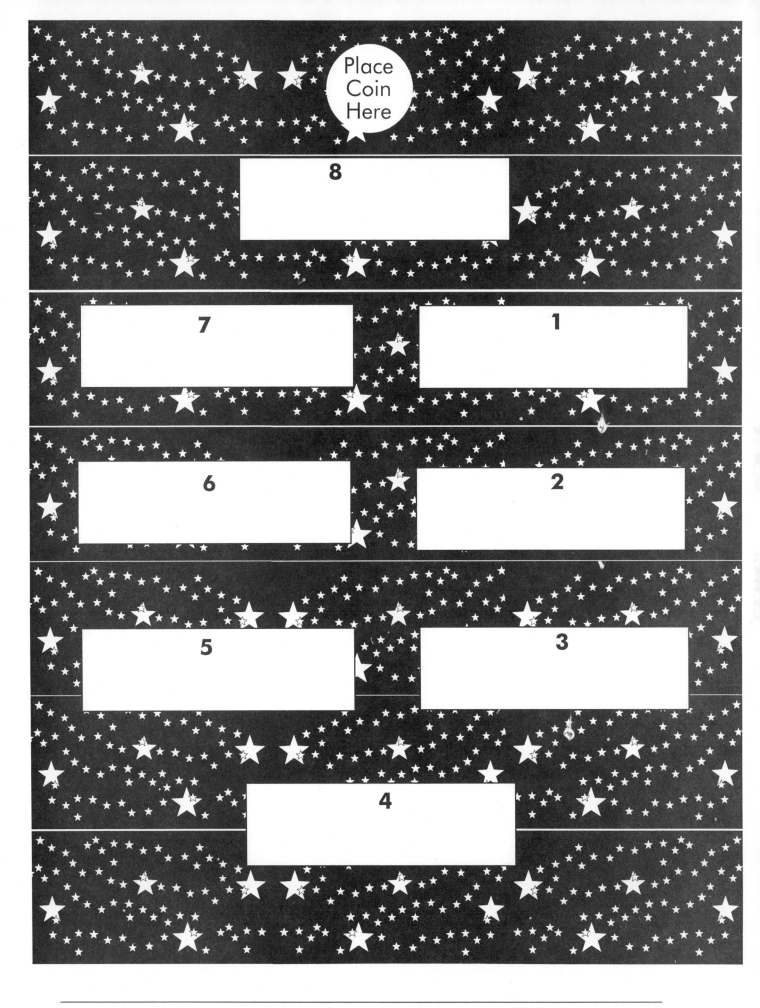

HOP TO IT!

"Let's hop to it!" is really illustrated by this simple origami fold that's fun and easy to teach! By simply following the instructions on the back of the handout, each person finishes with a giant paper frog that really jumps!

Directions

To make the frog jump, press down on and allow your finger to slip off of the rear end of the frog.

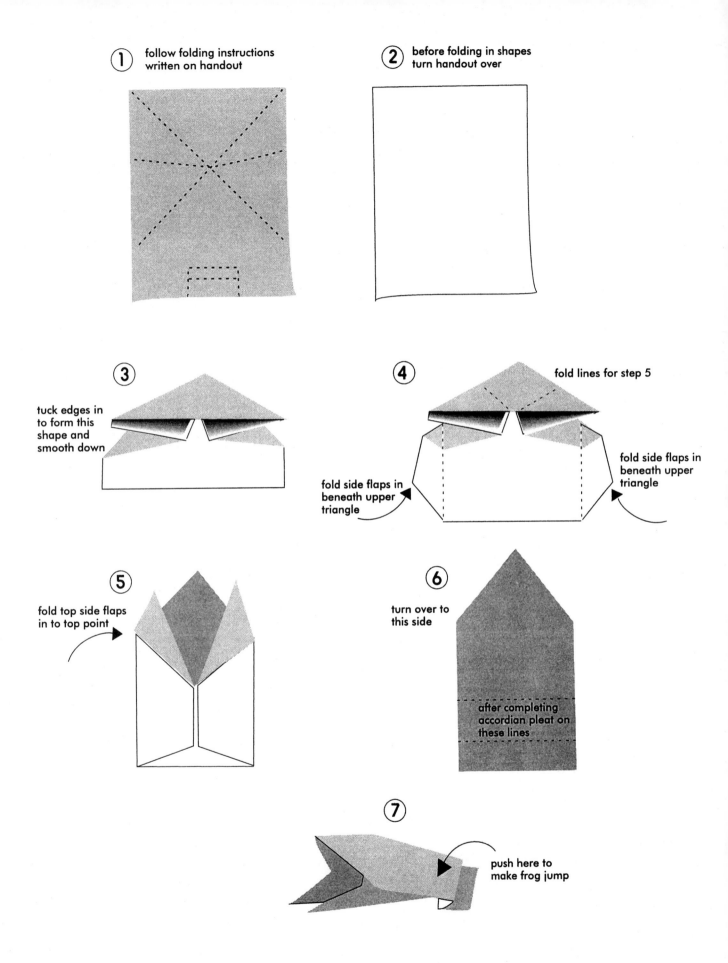

① follow folding instructions written on handout

② before folding in shapes turn handout over

③ tuck edges in to form this shape and smooth down

④ fold lines for step 5

fold side flaps in beneath upper triangle

fold side flaps in beneath upper triangle

⑤ fold top side flaps in to top point

⑥ turn over to this side

after completing accordian pleat on these lines

⑦ push here to make frog jump

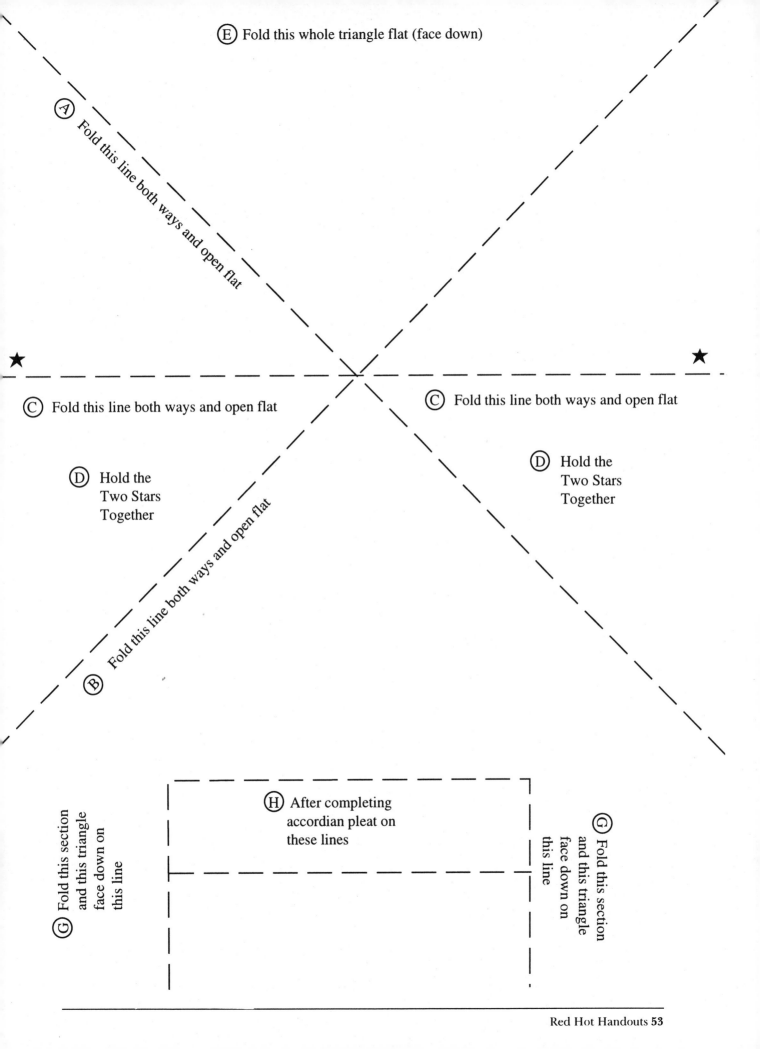

Ⓔ Fold this whole triangle flat (face down)

Ⓐ Fold this line both ways and open flat

★

★

Ⓒ Fold this line both ways and open flat

Ⓒ Fold this line both ways and open flat

Ⓓ Hold the Two Stars Together

Ⓓ Hold the Two Stars Together

Ⓑ Fold this line both ways and open flat

Ⓖ Fold this section and this triangle face down on this line

Ⓗ After completing accordian pleat on these lines

Ⓖ Fold this section and this triangle face down on this line

Red Hot Handouts 53

(F) Fold on the line towards you

(F) Fold on the line towards you

AIRBORNE

Do you have trouble with your trainees returning evaluations? Not anymore! Duplicate these lines onto the back of your evaluations and your participants can fly them to the front of the room! Each handout becomes a paper airplane! An additional idea for training transfer is also included with this template.

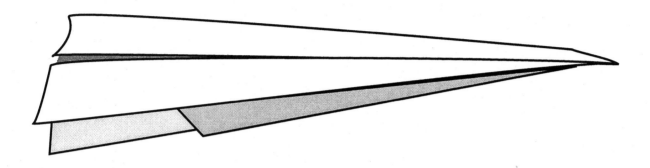

Directions

Besides using this activity for sending evaluations to the front of the room, consider using the following paper airplane template for training transfer. Use this paper airplane template for training transfer by having individuals write letters to themselves on the back of the template about how they hope to apply the content they just received in training.

Give them time to fold their planes and then fly them around the room — picking up and flying others two or three times.

Then have them pick up a plane close to them and read what the person wrote. They are to contact that person in two weeks to see how they're doing in their desired application of content.

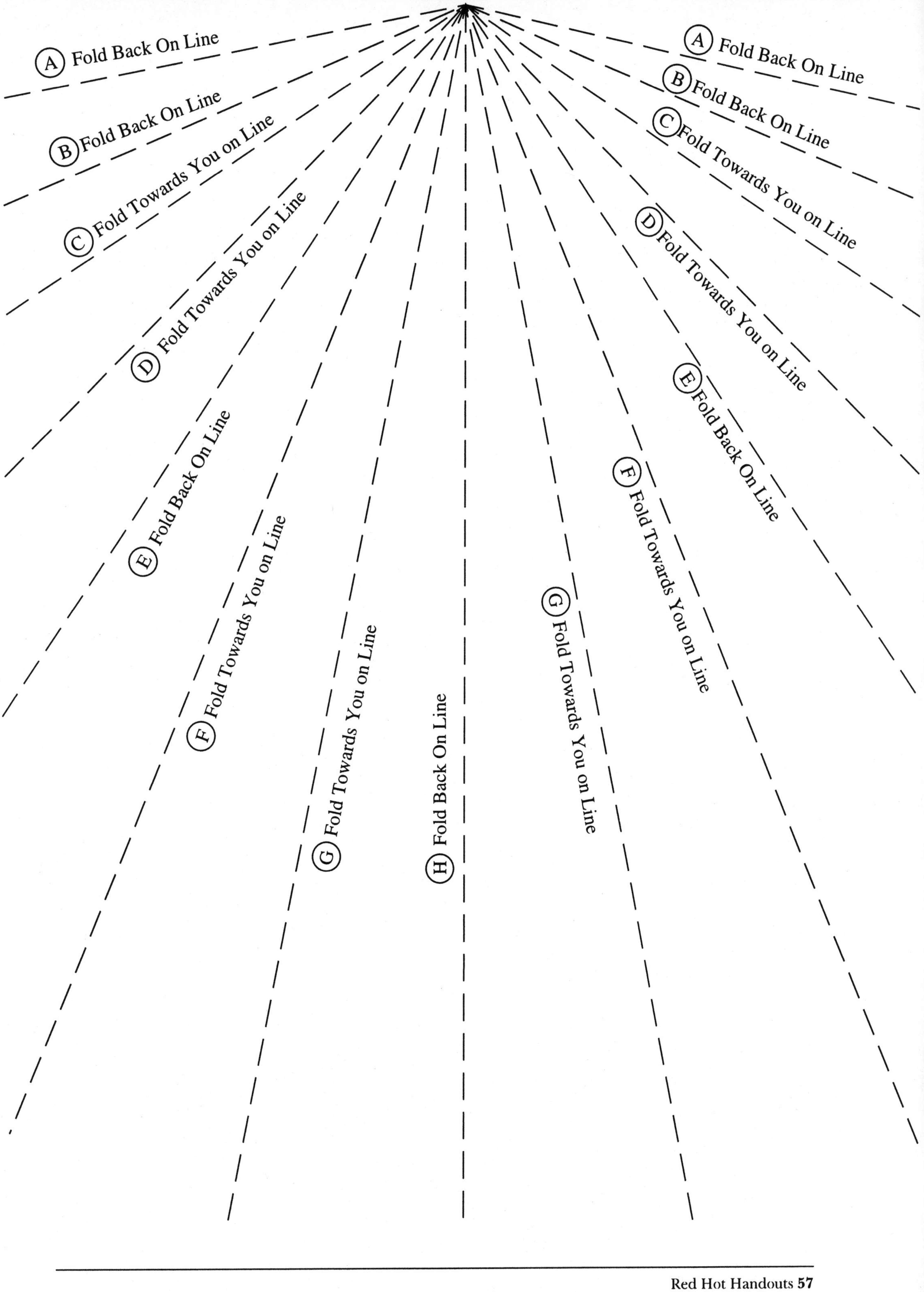
A Fold Back On Line
B Fold Back On Line
C Fold Towards You on Line
D Fold Towards You on Line
E Fold Back On Line
F Fold Towards You on Line
G Fold Towards You on Line
H Fold Back On Line
G Fold Towards You on Line
F Fold Towards You on Line
E Fold Back On Line
D Fold Towards You on Line
C Fold Towards You on Line
B Fold Back On Line
A Fold Back On Line

AeroDynamic

Turn any handout into an old airplane with wings that really flap! "Any idea can carry you somewhere!" is the slogan proudly painted on the airplane's side. This is excellent for reminding every participant how we can always build on even the silliest ideas!

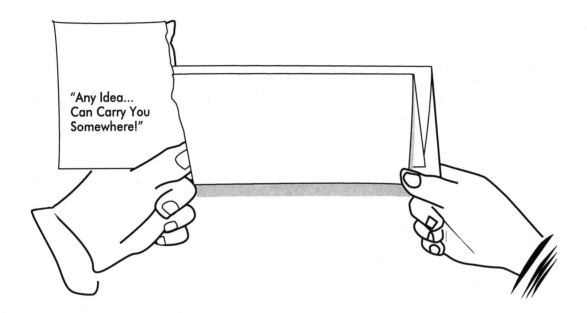

"Any Idea...
Can Carry You
Somewhere!"

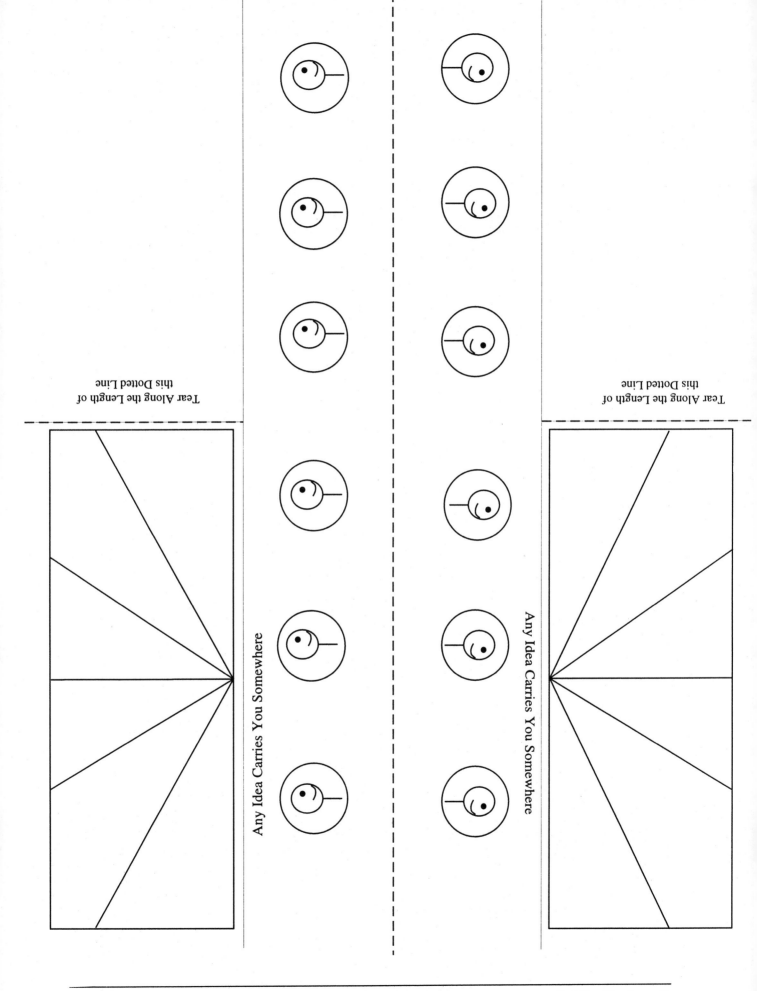

ON YOUR MARK!

With a few folds, this handout becomes a race's starter pistol! When everyone fires their guns, a special content summary message appears at the end of each gun barrel!

bang!

Directions

After folding the template, grip it by the very tip of the dark tabs with the arrow pointing down.

Move your arm quickly down in a chopping motion, and your summarizing message should pop out in a loud snapping sound!

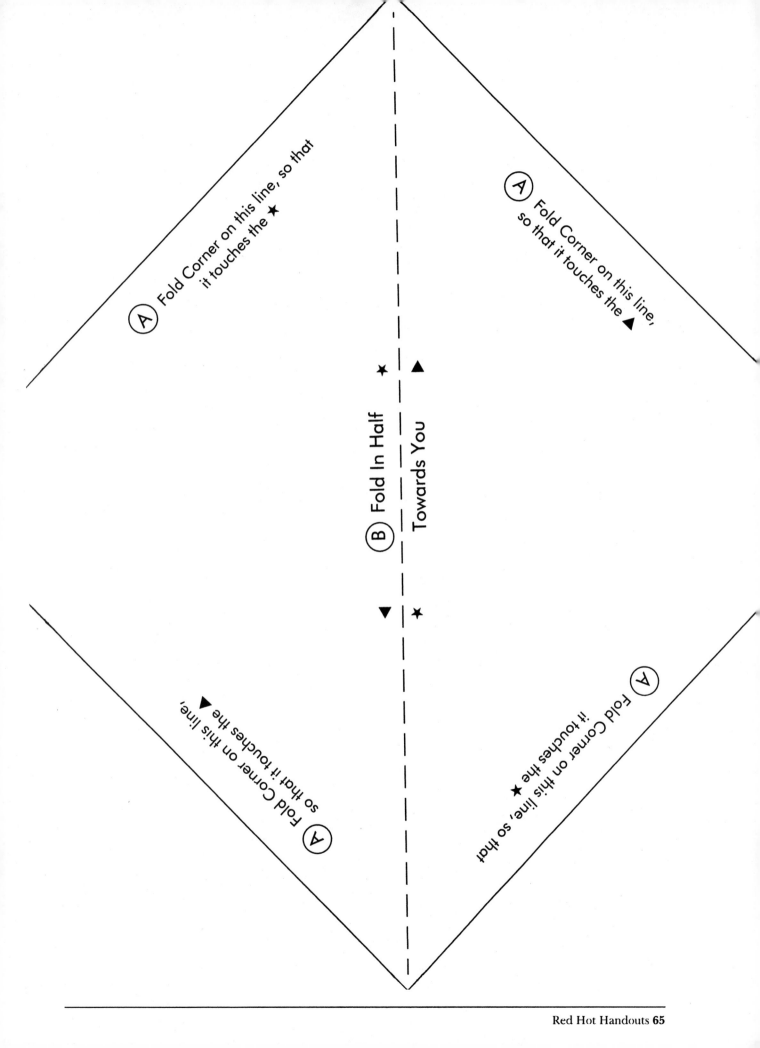

Ⓐ Fold Corner on this line, so that it touches the ★

Ⓐ Fold Corner on this line, so that it touches the ▲

Ⓑ Fold In Half

Towards You

Ⓐ Fold Corner on this line, so that it touches the ▲

Ⓐ Fold Corner on this line, so that it touches the ★

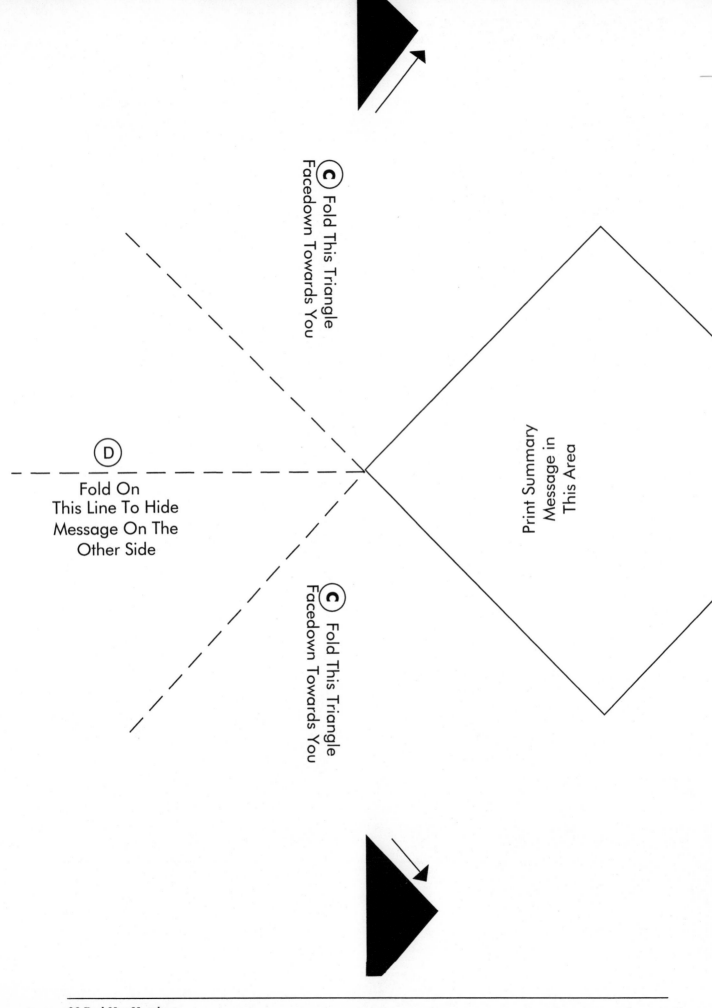

Ⓒ Fold This Triangle
Facedown Towards You

Ⓓ Fold On
This Line To Hide
Message On The
Other Side

Print Summary
Message in
This Area

Ⓒ Fold This Triangle
Facedown Towards You

INSTANT SEPARATION

This handout works best when covering positive and negative aspects of any subject. Sixteen different areas can be emphasized. Then when each person folds their handout into sixteenths (making each fold any direction the person wants), cuts around all four edges of the packet (through all thicknesses of the paper), and deals with the resultant face-up pieces into one pile and the face-down pieces into another; the positive qualities will be in one pile and negative qualities in the other! It's unbelievable to see the separation work!

Directions

In building your handout using the following template, place the negative qualities in squares 1, 3, 6, 8, 9, 11, 14, 16 and the positive qualities in squares 2, 4, 5, 7, 10, 12, 13, 15. Then when the above description is followed, the negative and positive aspects will indeed have been separated.

Each participant can make each fold any direction he or she wants!

1)

2)

3)

4)

5)

6)

7)

8)

9)

10)

11)

12)

13)

14)

15)

16)

COIN TOSS

This handout becomes an instant carnival game for great review! It's an excellent energizer for team play!

Directions

After filling in the individual squares with content, have everyone at a table stand, take a coin and toss it onto the handout (from about one foot away).

Each person must summarize for the others at the table the area into which most of their coin landed!

THE COIN TOSS

A Star Is Born

The trainer folds his or her handout and with one snip of the scissors, transforms it into a perfectly formed star. Or you might consider printing this template on the back of a "Course Graduation Certificate." At the conclusion of the course have all your participants fold their own certificate with you and tear out the star. Then we can say, "You'll help everyone believe that your training can help make everyone stars!" It's a great closer for any training session.

Directions

Print the following template onto the back of your own handout.

Use the lines as a guide for folding and cut across all thicknesses where indicated.

You'll help everyone believe that your training can help make everyone stars!

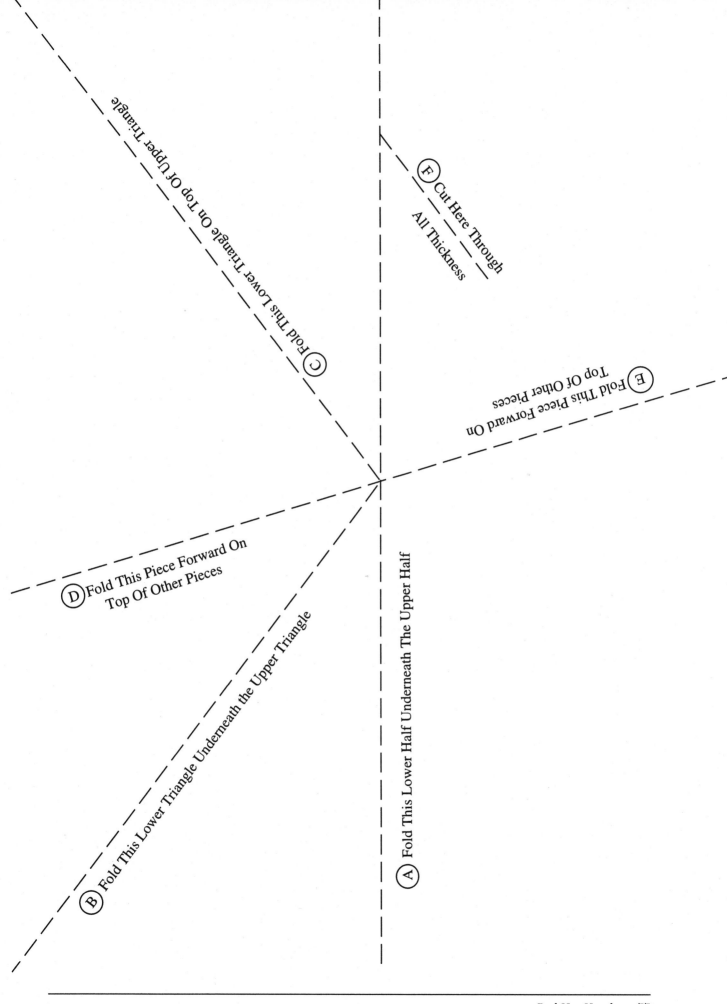

C — Fold This Lower Triangle On Top Of Upper Triangle

F — Cut Here Through All Thickness

E — Fold This Piece Forward On Top Of Other Pieces

D — Fold This Piece Forward On Top Of Other Pieces

B — Fold This Lower Triangle Underneath the Upper Triangle

A — Fold This Lower Half Underneath The Upper Half

CAPTURE THE CONTENT!

Watch your outline become a reinforcing game at the conclusion of your session.

Directions

Throughout your presentation, have participants insert your key emphases inside the boxes of the following gameboard. However, make sure you place your summarizing (most important concept) in the triangular square.

The secret to winning everytime is to be the first player to move once completely around the perimeter of this upper right-hand corner triangular square **before chasing the other person.** Try it with this strategy and you'll win everytime! If you don't use this strategy, you'll never capture the content.

After letting your participants play the game once or twice, share this secret strategy with them, and you will have emphasized the importance of whatever content piece you had placed in the upper right-hand corner triangle.

With a few modifications, this also works well as a game entitled **Catch the Competition!**

Capture the Content

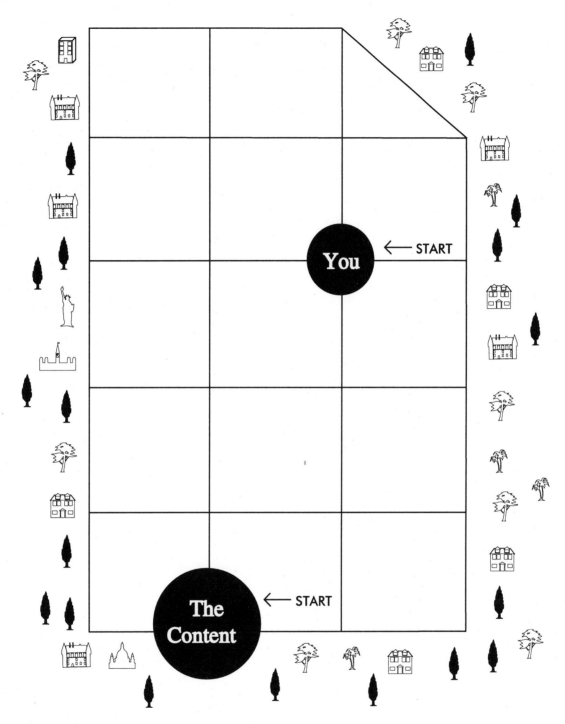

1. Put a large coin on the Content's starting circle and a small coin on your (the "You") starting circle.

2. Two people play. You always move first. Then players alternate turns.

3. Each move is one block in any direction.

4. You try to capture the Content. This is accomplished by moving the smaller coin so that it finally lands on top of the larger coin. Your opponent attempts to keep the Content away from you.

5. If the Content isn't captured in 50 of your moves, the Content wins that round.

HOLDING WATER

Do your content ideas hold water? Good question! However, when your participants finish folding your handout, they will have a paper cup that can actually hold water!

Holding Water Finished Product

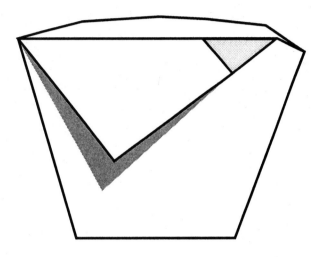

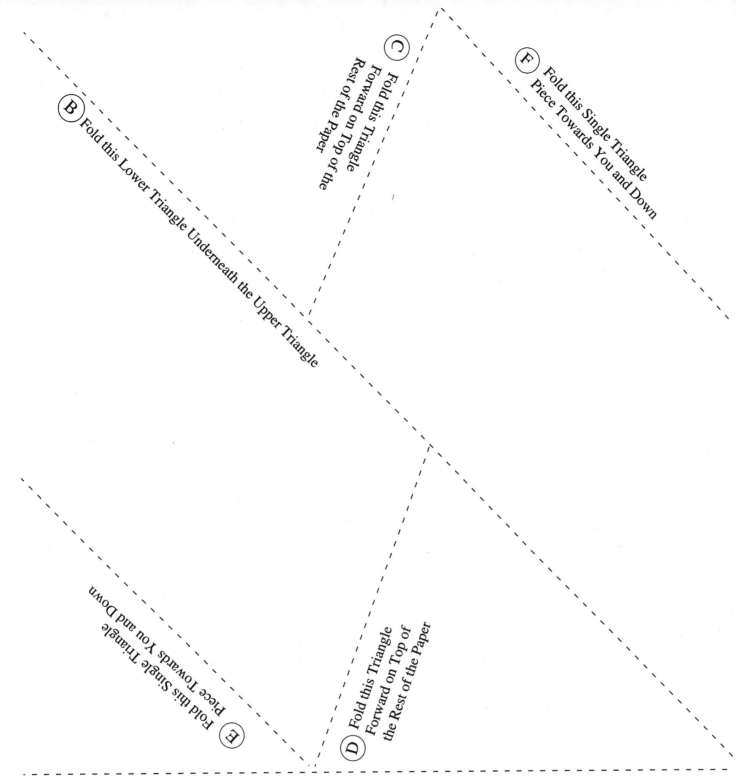

(B) Fold this Lower Triangle Underneath the Upper Triangle

(C) Fold this Triangle Forward on Top of the Rest of the Paper

(F) Fold this Single Triangle Piece Towards You and Down

(E) Fold this Single Triangle Piece Towards You and Down

(D) Fold this Triangle Forward on Top of the Rest of the Paper

(A) Fold this Lower Rectangle Underneath

PRIZES!

Print this number grid and prize listing on the back of your handout and then use it to review content. Each person circles different numbers in the grid to select one of the prizes...and amazingly enough, although everyone selects different numbers, they lead everyone to winning the SAME PRIZE! The trainer controls which prize everyone wins! A great activity to use just before break!

Directions

Simply have participants fill in the four blank boxes on the following template with review content.

Then follow the instructions, and everyone will win a Paperclip Keychain (#34) every time!

Have a box of paperclips ready and show them how neatly a person can use one to hold their keys together!

Prizes!

	1	2	3	4
	5	6	7	8
	9	10	11	12
	13	14	15	16

Directions

Print the key emphasis of the presentation in any order into the four empty boxes at the left of each row. Then circle any number in the top row (1–4) and draw a line down the column underneath it—eliminating all those numbers in the column underneath—eliminating all those numbers in the column underneath your selected number. Proceed to circle any number in the second row (5–8) that hasn't been eliminated and draw a line down from it eliminating the numbers underneath it, too. Continue in the same manner with the third row (9–12) and the fourth row (13–16). Add the circled numbers to find your prize!

1. $5,000 Cash
2. World Cruise
3. Computer
4. Fax Machine
5. Round Trip Airfare To Any U.S. City
6. Entertainment Center
7. Porsche
8. Classical CD Collection
9. Private Airplane
10. Chauffeur For One Year
11. Limousine
12. Vacation Home
13. Lincoln Continental
14. Hawaiian Vacation
15. Dinner For Two
16. $1,500 Gift Certificate
17. Answering Machine
18. $2,000 Cash

19. Beach Front Property
20. European Vacation
21. Lexus
22. Free Gasoline For One Year
23. Classic Movie Videos
24. King Size Waterbed
25. Home Jacuzzi
26. Home Swimming Pool
27. $1,500 Mall Shopping Spree
28. Portable CD Player
29. Laptop Computer
30. Sailboat
31. $3,000 Wardrobe
32. Home Intercom System
33. Cellular Phone
34. Paper Clip Key Chain
35. Free Cellular Phone Service
36. Movie Passes

PRIZES! PRIZES!

Still another way to work the previous review and prize giveaway to bring even greater variety into your training session!

Directions

Print this template on the back of your handout. At the conclusion of your session, let participants fill in the blank boxes in the grid with content emphases. Then if they follow the instructions they will all win a Paperclip Keychain (#65) every time!

Be ready with a box of paperclips and show them how a key fits on one quite nicely!

Prizes! Prizes!

	1	2	3	4	5
	6	7	8	9	10
	11	12	13	14	15
	16	17	18	19	20
	21	22	23	24	25

Directions

Print the main emphases of the presentation in any order in the boxes on the far left end of each row. Print the same emphases in any order in the boxes across the top of each column. Place your index fingers on each of the mates from the left-hand boxes and the top—bringing your fingers down and across until they meet. Circle that number. Do this for each of the emphases. Add the five circled numbers to find your prize in the list below!

1. $5,000 Cash
2. World Cruise
3. Computer
4. Fax Machine
5. Round Trip Airfare To Any U.S. City
6. Entertainment Center
7. Porsche
8. Classical CD Collection
9. Private Airplane
10. Chauffeur For One Year
11. Limousine
12. Vacation Home
13. Lincoln Continental
14. Hawaiian Vacation
15. Dinner For Two
16. $1,500 Gift Certificate
17. Answering Machine
18. $2,000 Cash
19. Condominium
20. Aspen Ski Vacation
21. Home Landscaping ($5,000)
22. Maid Service for One Year
23. Yacht
24. Beach Front Property

25. European Vacation
26. Lexus
27. Free Gasoline for One Year
28. Classic Movie Videos
29. King Size Waterbed
30. Home Jacuzzi
31. Home Swimming Pool
32. $1,500 Mall Shopping Spree
33. Portable CD Player
34. Laptop Computer
35. Sailboat
36. $3,000 Wardrobe
37. Home Intercom System
38. Cellular Phone
39. Living Room Furniture
40. Free Cellular Phone Service
41. Movie Passes
42. Home Cleaning Products
43. Two Servants for One Year
44. Alaskan Cruise
45. Jamaican Holiday
46. Patio Furniture
47. Broadway Shows
48. Super Bowl Trip
49. One Year's Salary

50. Townhouse
51. Rental Property
52. $500 Makeover
53. Date With a Star!
54. $5,000 IRA Account
55. $500 Savings Bond
56. South America Trip
57. Disneyland Trip
58. Lawn Furniture
59. Big Screen TV
60. African Photo Safari
61. Screened Deck
62. Extra Paid Vacation
63. A Salary Increase
64. Stun Gun
65. Paperclip Keychain
66. Free Long Distance
67. Far Eastern Trip
68. $900 Cash
69. Lottery Ticket

ACTION GRAPHICS

This section contains 26 graphics for adding action to any handout —
increasing participant interaction and retention!

FLYING HIGH

Watch the airplane in this artwork slowly turn right before your eyes. Great for emphasizing change. Just copy it onto your handout and watch the fun!

Take a moment to study the following graphic and try to determine the direction that the lower-most plane is flying.

Now cover the plane in the upper left-hand corner with one of your hands and watch the lower plane turn. Now remove your hand from the plane in the upper left-hand corner and cover the plane in the upper right-hand corner and watch the lower plane turn again.

The lower plane seems to align itself with whichever plane is most dominant in the picture! That's the power inherent in being a change agent!

THE WRITING ON THE WALL

You can make your trainees see your summarizing message floating in the air around the room. Here's how! Works excellent with any content!

In 1866, a London publisher produced a small booklet entitled *"Spectropia"* with a subtitle of *"Surprising Spectral Illusions Showing Ghosts Everywhere And Of Any Colour."*

Throughout the booklet were pictures of ghosts and skeletons that the reader was instructed to stare at for twenty to thirty seconds. Then whenever the reader looked at a blank white wall, the ghost would be seen floating in the air in front of that wall!

And the ghost would be in a contrasting color to the ghost in the book. If the ghost was white in the booklet, it would be black when seen in the air and vice versa.

If the ghost was red in the booklet, it would be blue in the air and so on.

Try it yourself with the following graphic!

Stare at very top point on the letter L for 20-30 seconds, trying not to blink. Then lift your eyes and look towards a white wall surface in the room. In the training room, the overhead projector screen works great! Blink several times.

Now select a graphic or word that summarizes your content session. Print it in a sharply contrasting manner as above. Then you're ready to finish your session with an experience your participants will not soon forget! Be sure to have them stare at only one central point in your graphic. One of the best by-products of this activity is this — each time your participants try it again or show it to a friend, more training transfer occurs!

VANISHING ART

Here's how to make any handout graphic vanish right before each of your trainees' eyes! Many applications!

Close your right eye and hold this page approximately ten inches away from your eyes and stare hard at the $ sign (on the right). Slowly move the book from side to side, keeping your eye fixed on the face. Suddenly the customer's face will disappear! That's how it often is when we make the profit the focus of our attention rather than focusing on customer service!

It works because each one of us does indeed have a "blind spot" in our eyes where the optic nerve joins the retina. At that location there are no "rods" or "cones" and, consequently, an inability to see light rays or color.

Use this pattern to substitute any content-oriented items you can imagine!

Anything you want to make disappear can with this illustration!

COME IN!

Use this one on your next handout and watch your participants really come alive! A bird and a cage are seen in a picture right next to each other. Yet as the group follows your instructions, they watch the bird slowly walk into the cage! Use your imagination to customize this to your content with any two pictures of your choice dramatically coming together! Two additional graphics included for differing applications.

Hold the following graphic at a normal reading distance. Put a plain index card at a 90 degree angle to the graphic along the dotted line. Then slowly bring the graphic closer to your face. You'll watch the bird walk into the cage!

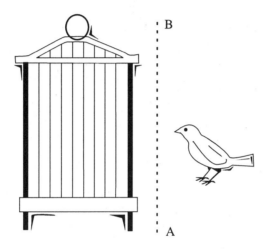

If you try it with the following graphic, you'll watch the customer walk into the store!

Using the same procedure, you'll now see the dollar sign enter the company.

Now try designing an Action Graphic for your handout specific to your own content!

TRIANGULAR!

How many triangles can your trainees find in this piece of modern art? There are always more than anyone first suspects! That's how it is with most learning too! There's more to any subject than anyone first anticipates!

Copy the following artwork onto your handout, and ask your participants to guess the number of triangles within its borders.

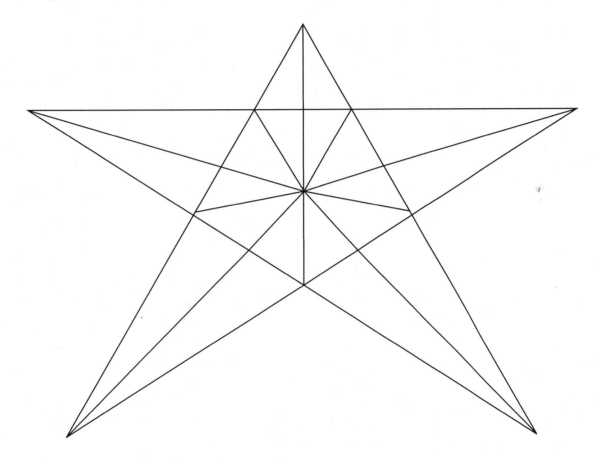

The actual total is 97 triangles! The more you look at any subject the more facets you see!

TIC-TAC-TOE TOP SECRET

Decorate your handout with this tic-tac-toe border and demonstrate how important having a system is to winning anything! Imagine never losing at tic-tac-toe even though you play blindfolded — never seeing where the other person places their mark! That's exactly what you do as you illustrate how many things become possible once a system has been mastered!

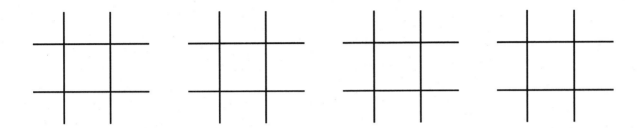

You must learn the following simple process before trying to play tic-tac-toe blindfolded.

In order for this system to work, you must be first to play. That won't be a difficult concession for your opponent to give you since you are willing to play the game blindfolded — never seeing where he or she puts his mark!

First, try the simple system without the blindfold. Let's say that you have the Xs and your opponent has the Os. Always begin by puting your X put in the center square.

Your opponent will then put an O in one of the remaining empty squares.

Each time you get ready to place your X, follow these easy steps:

1) If the square is empty to the RIGHT of your opponent's O, put your X there.

2) If that square is taken and the square is empty to the LEFT of your opponent's O, put your X there.

3) If that square is also taken and the square is empty ABOVE your opponent's O, put your X there.

4) And if that square is also taken, then finally put your X put BELOW your opponent's O.

Each time you get ready to place your X, use the O your opponent just marked and go through your options in the order listed above (RIGHT-LEFT-ABOVE-BELOW). You will never lose! If you opponent makes a judgment error, you might even win!

Directions

You'll need to have a blackboard, flip chart, or overhead so that others can see you play your opponent. Participants can play along at their desks.

Bring someone to the front to play the game with you. Draw a large tic-tac-toe grid and put your X in the middle.

Put on your blindfold and turn your back to the board before continuing the game.

Allow your opponent to put an O anywhere he or she wants. Then follow in order the four steps of the strategy until you hit an open square and have him or her put your X there. Then place your opponent's next O and you keep alternating with your opponent until the game is either won by you or comes to a draw! You will usually draw on the fifth X you place.

Why not really make this sensational and put on your blindfold ready to play the entire group of participants all at the same time! As long as they let you begin (with an X in the middle) and follow your instructions explicitly, you shouldn't lose to any of them!

Many impossibilities become possible with a good plan!

FINGER PLAY

In this artwork, the participants bring the graphic to life as their fingers become ears! It's a riot!

Duplicate the following graphic onto your handout. When you're ready to make the demonstration come alive, have your participants cut out the dark circles.

Then each participant needs to extend their index and middle fingers using both hands behind the handout and putting those fingers through the holes in the graphic.

Their fingers have become ears for the graphic figures! By extending their middle fingers towards each other, they will cause the figures to reach out and join ears as a symbol of teamwork!

By using your imagination, you can make other Action Graphics to fit your content in which fingers become legs and even arms.

A HOME RUN

Watch the baseball slowly move in a home run arch right into the glove! A golf ball graphic magically dropping into the hole is also included.

Copy this next graphic onto your handout and instruct your participants to put their nose on the dot. By rotating the page counterclockwise the ball will appear to arc into the glove. You've caught a home run!

Great for emphasizing the fact that we can all be winners!

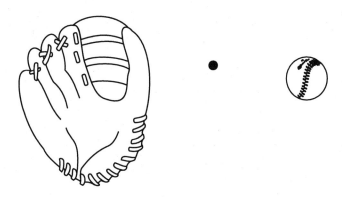

Copy this graphic onto your handout and instruct your participants to put their nose halfway between the hole and the ball. By rotating the page counterclockwise the ball will appear to drop into the hole. You've made a hole in one!

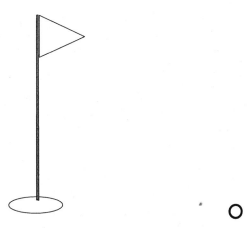

Here's another idea! Use the distance between the two items in either picture as your formula and then build a graphic to uniquely fit your own content!

AN EYE OPENER

The lady in this graphic slowly and mysteriously opens her eyes as you watch her!

Copy this graphic onto your handout and be ready to amaze! Watch her eyes and they will slowly open and look at you!

We often see what we're told to see! Expectations often help determine results!

CENTERED

Is the dot in the middle of this triangle? You'll never know for sure without measuring! Content can surround the triangle on this handout!

Copy the following piece of artwork onto your handout. As suggested in the description, you might consider placing it in the center.

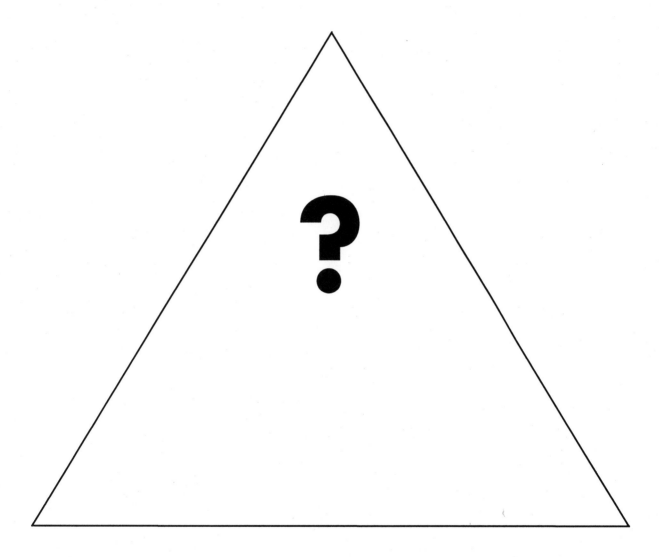

Now is the dot of the question mark in the center of the triangle, a little high of center, or a little low? If you take time to measure, you will find that the dot of the question mark is exactly in the center between the base and the apex!

What a dramatic way to show how wrong our initial assessments of any situation can be! Without careful consideration, the decision-making process is flawed.

TIGHTROPE WALK

This poor tightrope walker's rope has broken! Watch it magically come together right before your eyes! Two other versions are included for differing applications!

Try this! Hold the following graphic at normal reading distance and then bring the graphic closer to your face until your nose is between the piece of broken rope. You'll watch the rope coming together on the page!

Using the same procedure, you'll see the fragmented team unified again!

Or, you'll also see the bridge repaired and people saved!

Now try to design an Action Graphic specific to your content!

PENDULUM PAPER

The chart on the handout brings each pendulum to life as the trainer asks specific questions — causing the individual pendulums to move in response! It's spooky!

In *Tricks For Trainers, Volume I*, a pendulum is used to demonstrate our suggestibility. Basically, each participant tied a key or ring to one end of about an 18" length of string or yarn.

By pinching the other end between their index finger and thumb, the article would hang suspended by the string. By standing up and extending their arm from their body, each person's article hung freely in space.

As the trainer began talking about the articles moving in a circle, the articles would indeed begin rotating at the end of their strings. This is made possible by the nearly imperceptible ideomotor movement of each person's arm in response to the suggestions made by the trainer. The participants will usually not be aware of such movement, and the articles seem to take on a life of their own!

As an expansion of this theme, the following graphic gives a guide for interpreting the movement of the pendulum. As the pendulum moves from the left to right, it is indicating a NO answer to the question posed by the trainer. As the pendulum moves from up to down (vertical as in the shaking of the head), it indicates a YES answer to the question of the trainer.

Thus by asking summarizing or simple review questions, the pendulum will now respond to YES or NO questions. Give it a try!

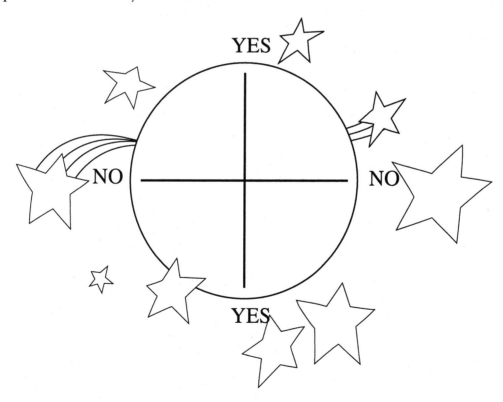

EMPLOYMENT TEST

Through a cute story and this artwork, the trainer explains how the company's luckiest job applicant got hired! Of course, the real name of that employee will always remain a secret!

Copy the following artwork onto your handout, and you'll be ready to tell your story!

OFFICIAL

EMPLOYMENT TEST

Math Competencies

Part One: Geometry

Divide this box into four equal parts.

Part Two: Multiplication

Complete the following:

2 x 9 = _____

3 X 9 = _____

4 x 9 = _____

5 x 9 = _____

6 x 9 = _____

7 x 9 = _____

8 x 9 = _____

9 x 9 = _____

You might want to make a transparency of the artwork for use in telling your story. Then you could be filling in the test as you relate the employee's actions.

You're now ready to tell the story about the luckiest job applicant in the company's history.

"He came in to take the math portion of his employment testing and looked at the test and just passed by the first part regarding Geometry. He didn't even know the meaning of the word!

However, he didn't know any of the answers to the rest of the exam either. He thought to himself, 'I wonder how many I'm going to miss?' He numbered them as he counted."

Beginning with the 2 x 9 blank, you number down the column 1...2...3...4...5...6...7...8 with one digit in the blank beside each math problem.

"'Oh, no,' he thought, 'I'm going to miss 8! Wait a minute! Maybe I miscounted!' So he counted them again."

This time you start with the 9 x 9 problem at the bottom and number up the chart. Place each number in the blank to the right of the number you've already placed there.

"'1...2...3...4...5...6...7...8! I'm really going to miss eight!' the man said to himself."

Your participants will begin to see that the test is now completed perfectly! However, don't wait for a response. Just go on!

"'No, wait,' the man thought, 'I'm going to miss nine! I have no idea about this Geometry question!' With that he crossed out the box by putting a big X inside of it from corner to corner!"

To illustrate what you have just said, you now draw an X in the box.

"The man was shocked when the test came back with a perfect score, and he got the job!"

Here is an example of the finished product.

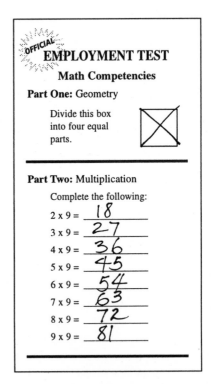

THE IMPOSSIBLE HOLE

What's that hole doing in the handout? A dime size hole in the handout looks too small to have a quarter go through it...but it's not! Many things only look impossible!

Copy the following dime-size hole (.75 inches in diameter) onto your handout about one finger length from an edge. Have your participants carefully cut away all the black from the circle.

The challenge is simple. Each participant needs to figure out how to push a quarter through the small hole without tearing the paper. Show them how much smaller the diameter of the hole is in relation to the diameter of the quarter by laying a quarter flat over the hole.

Surely someone will try the old gag of putting their finger through the hole and then pushing the quarter along the tabletop. Probably that does indeed qualify as "pushing the quarter through the hole." However, it really is possible to actually put the quarter through the hole without tearing the paper!

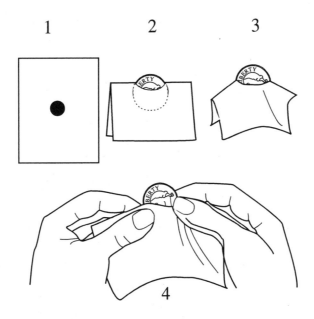

Take the handout and fold it so that the fold runs right through the diameter of the hole. Then put the quarter into the folded paper so that it rests in the hole. By simultaneously pushing gently on the quarter and pulling outwards and upwards on the sides of the circle, you will find that the quarter can now be pushed gently right through the dime-size hole!

THE TRICK THAT FOOLED EINSTEIN

This magic trick actually fooled the great scientist, Albert Einstein! A prediction is printed on the handout and seen by all ahead of time. A handful of small content-oriented items (possibly coins) is grabbed from a pile by a volunteer from the audience. When the prediction is read, it foretells exactly the number of items the volunteer selected. It can then be repeated with a different prediction and a different result. Great for starting a group talking about possible solutions to this trick! Gets them truly involved in a problem-solving frame of mind.

In preparation for this demonstration, obtain 200 pennies. Put 101 pennies in an empty jar and 90 pennies in an open bowl. You won't need the other nine cents for this experiment.

Copy the following prediction onto your handout.

MY JAR CONTAINS AS MANY PENNIES AS THE
TOTAL NUMBER OF PENNIES ALL OF
YOU TOOK PLUS TWELVE MORE WITH
ENOUGH LEFT OVER TO MAKE YOUR
PENNIES TOTAL 101.

When you're ready for this demonstration, pass around the bowl of 90 pennies and let each person take as many as they wish — leaving as many in the bowl as they wish.

They must then add together to determine the total number of pennies they all took. Holding up your jar of pennies, you're ready to prove the truth of your uncanny prediction.

By way of example, let's say the group took a total of 64 pennies from the bowl.

First you said that you'd have "as many pennies as the total number of pennies all of you took." Consequently, count 64 pennies from your jar.

Then you said that you'd have "12 more." Therefore, count 12 more pennies from your jar. Indicate that you now have a total of 78 pennies.

But you also said that you would then have "enough left over to make your pennies total 101." Beginning with the number 79, count the pennies remaining in your jar and you'll find that, indeed, you will reach the number 101 with the very last penny.

Some may soon figure out that the solution to this puzzle lies in the very confusing wording of your prediction. All your prediction really says is that you have one hundred and one pennies in your jar. As long as the bowl contains less than 89 pennies (101 pennies minus 12 pennies), the prediction will always be correct.

It is a wonderful illustration of the power of printed communication to amaze and confuse!

FINGER TALK

Everyone experiences this one together as the trainer asks them to each move one finger or another in response to a series of lesson questions. Imagine their surprise when they all find themselves unable to move one of their fingers even though they all want to!

Copy the following graphic onto your handout.

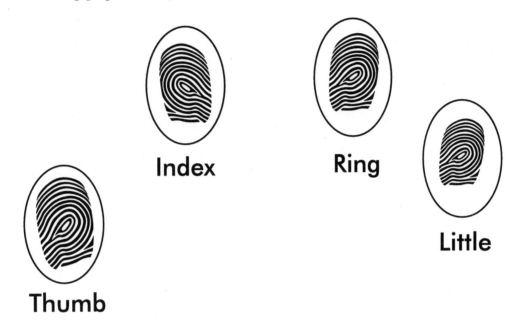

Index   Ring

Little

Thumb

When you're ready for this exercise, have everyone put their fingertips into the appropriate finger print on their handout. Since there is not a place for the middle finger, they need to curl that finger underneath their hand so that the tip of their middle finger touches the palm of their hand.

With their hands in that position, you are now going to ask them a series of questions:

1) "If you wished you won 17 million dollars in the lottery, wiggle your thumb."

   You will see thumbs wiggling throughout the room.

2) "If you wished you had six months of paid vacation every year, wiggle your index finger."

   Index fingers will be waving at you throughout the room.

3) "If you wished you were going to get a 30% raise this year, please wiggle your little finger."

   Little fingers should now be waving.

4) "If you wished you had to spend less time training with me, please wiggle your ring finger."

   No ring fingers should be wiggling. It's a physical impossibility with the hand in that position.

However, you should act surprised and come back with a comment like, "I didn't know you cared!"

Obviously, the questions can be tailored more specifically to content. I'm sure you get the idea.

ALPHABET SOUP

This teaches you how to customize a classic observation test to your own content! Applicable to any content!

The following is a classic observation test. The rules are simple. Read through the following paragraph only once — counting the number of Fs in the paragraph:

FINISHED FILES ARE THE RE-
SULT OF YEARS OF SCIENTIF-
IC STUDY COMBINED WITH
THE EXPERIENCE OF YEARS.

Most will find three Fs in the sentence. Few will find all six.

If we take a moment to analyze why this works, you will be able to use what we find to build a content-related paragraph to use in this exercise.

1) The first two words in the paragraph lead us to look for soft sounding Fs. The ones we miss are the Fs that sound like Vs in the word "of."

2) The improperly hyphenated word "scientific" gives further emphasis to the soft sounding F.

3) Finally, notice that the combination "of years" is repeated twice in the paragraph. Since we missed the F the first time, we are even more likely to miss it the second time.

Now you can use what you just learned to construct a paragraph for nearly any content topic. Here's one example for the theme of Customer Service:

FUN FRIENDLY EMPLOYEES ARE THE RE-
SULT OF YEARS OF SPECIF-
IC TRAINING COMBINED WITH
THE EXPERIENCE OF YEARS.

Have fun building one for your content!

WHEELING

This stationary circular design suddenly begins to rotate just like a wheel!

Copy the following artwork onto your handout and you're ready for the demonstration.

Although the circle obviously never moves, when your participants hold the handout in one hand and then move that hand in circular motions, the artwork appears to spin!

"We're really on a roll now," would be an appropriate comment.

It also very visually demonstrates the power of each person's perspective in what they ultimately see.

RIGHTSIDE UP!

Turn this graphic upside down and you won't believe the sudden change!

Below you'll see a whole pie with a piece removed — resting on a plate. However, if you turn the graphic upside down, you'll only see the piece! A person's unique perspective makes the difference in both of these graphics.

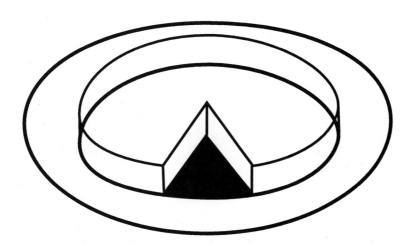

MAGIC SQUARES

Using a two-digit number randomly suggested by your participants at the beginning of your training session, progressively build this action graphic until you finish the session with a matrix of sixteen numbers that add together horizontally, vertically, diagonally and over 20 different directions to total the number first suggested by the group. Your trainees will be amazed, and you will have shown how amazing accomplishments can be when one is willing to take the time to design and follow a system.

Duplicate the following artwork on every handout, and you'll be ready to give a dynamic demonstration of how to work smarter not harder!

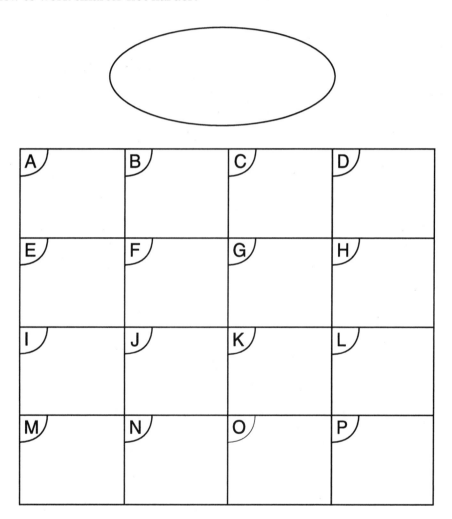

When ready to begin the demonstration, ask your participants to suggest a two digit number larger than 21. Upon receiving the number, have each person print that number in the oval at the top of the matrix.

Have the following prompter key secretly placed on your table so only you can see it. You are then ready to have your participants fill in the squares of their matrix with the numbers you're about to give them.

A	B	C	D
-20 "of the original two digit number"	**1**	**12**	**7**
E	F	G	H
11	**8**	**-1** "of the number in square A"	**2**
I	J	K	L
5	**10**	**3**	**+2** "of the number in square A"
M	N	O	P
4	**+1** "of the number in square A"	**6**	**9**

When you hear the group's two-digit number, first subtract 20 from that number and have your participants put the resulting difference into square A. Then read the numbers from the chart for squares B (1), C (12), D (7), E (11), and F (8). When you get to G, subtract 1 *from the number you placed in the A square.* Proceed to read off the numbers from the chart for the squares H (2), I (5), J (10), and K (3). For square L, give your participants a number that is 2 more than *the number you placed in the A square.*

Finally read the numbers from your prompter for the M (4) square adding one *to the number you placed in the A square* when you give them the N square number. Finish by giving the final two numbers from your prompter for the O (6) and P (9) squares.

Using this rather simple pattern, you will amaze yourself with the fact that you have now built a Magic Square in which the group's chosen two-digit number can be found by:

1) Adding together the numbers in any horizontal row.

2) Adding together the numbers in any vertical column.

3) Adding together the numbers in any diagonal row.

4) Adding together the numbers in any of the four corner quadrants.

5) Adding together the numbers in the middle grouping of four boxes (F, G, J, K).

6) As well as adding together numbers in boxes B, C, N, O or E, I, H, L.

7) Even the four outside corner boxes contain numbers that when added together will equal the chosen number (A, D, M, P)!

Something that incredible looks like it would take tremendous time and mental ability to put together. Really it only takes a well-thought-out plan. That's how it is with most incredible accomplishments!

After receiving the applause of your participants, take time to share the simplicity of the system with them. They'll appreciate your application even more! Training transfer is bound to also occur as they take the system and try it with their friends and family!

PITCHFORKED

How many prongs on this weird-looking pitchfork? Better count again! Our own beliefs change!

This classic optical illusion will really give your handout energy!

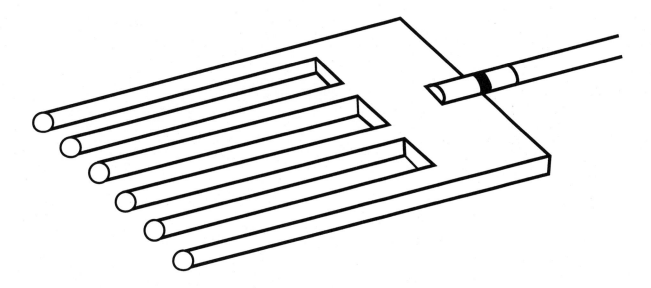

They can even debate it to try to prove the truth of their position. Ask your participants how many prongs they see. Very often there is more than one right answer!

HANDOUT HINTS

different proven ideas — bringing NEW life to any handout!

X-RAY TUBE

Sci-fi fans take note! Any handout becomes an x-ray tube. It will look exactly as though you can peer through your own hand when you use this tube!

Try this one yourself first! Take any handout and roll it into a long tube. Hold it up to one eye and *while keeping both eyes open* bring your empty hand alongside the tube with the open palm toward your face.

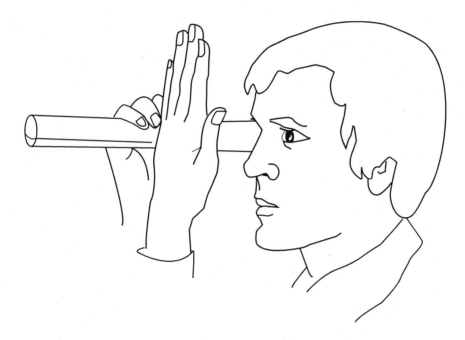

Move your open hand closer to your face and then farther away until you can apparently see right through a hole in your hand! Be sure to keep both eyes open as you do this!

Then teach your participants how to do it with their own handouts, and they won't soon forget how we can look at something very diligently and still not be sure about what we're seeing! The attitude of teachability is based upon just such an understanding.

STRIKE UP THE BAND

Any handout can be simply transformed into a flute that really plays! You and your participants will be making beautiful music in no time!

After taking their 8½" x 11" handout and folding up the bottom edge 2½" (so that they are now working with a square handout), have everyone roll their handout around a pencil — rolling from the lower left-hand corner to the upper right-hand corner. After removing the pencil, have them use a piece of clear cellophane tape to hold the tube together.

Look at the diagram below to see how to cut one end of the tube so that a reed is formed. If you've folded up one edge of your handout to make a square, then cut the end of the tube so that the reed is comprised of a single thickness of paper. You may need to cut away some paper to make this happen. The reed must lay flat on the open end of the tube for the flute to work.

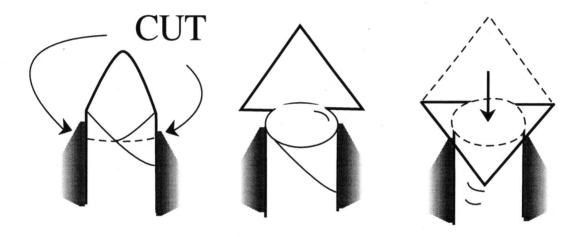

The secret is to *inhale* on the opposite end of the tube so that the paper reed is pulled against the end of the tube and vibrates against that opening. You will find your flute making a rather loud buzzing sound. The pitch of the buzzing is made higher or lower by cutting away pieces of the tube so that it becomes shorter and shorter.

When the entire room starts playing, it's quite an experience!

PAPER AND COIN DROP

The challenge is to drop a coin and a small piece of handout paper at the same time — having the paper reach the floor first. It can be done!

As you set up this challenge for your participants, tear a small piece of paper from your handout (the paper must be smaller than the diameter of a quarter). Hold that small piece in one hand and the quarter in the other hand. With arms outstretched, challenge your participants to come up with a way to drop the quarter and the paper at exactly the same time with the end result that the piece of paper reaches the floor first.

Have them tear off pieces from their handouts and try it at their tables with their own quarters.

One solution is to place the piece of paper underneath the quarter — dropping the quarter flatly down to the floor. Air pressure will push the piece of paper against the underside of the quarter with the result that the piece of paper will indeed reach the floor first.

The process of creativity in problem solving is a wonderful application for this exercise.

HANDOUT GRAB

The nervous system really gets a workout as a volunteer participant tries for a prize!

Have a volunteer come to the front of the room to help out in this experiment. Have the volunteer make a fist and then extend his or her thumb and index finger so that they are parallel to each other and parallel to the floor.

You hold the handout so that the halfway point of the handout's length is between the volunteer's thumb and index finger.

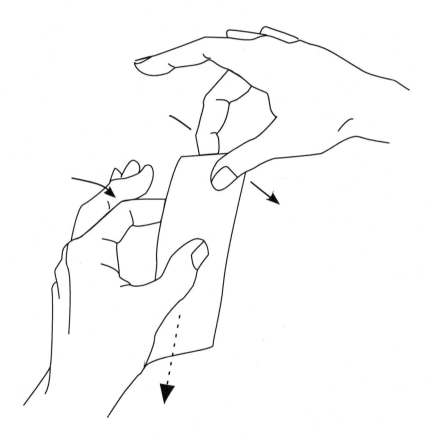

The challenge is for the volunteer to pinch the handout — stopping its fall when it is released by you the trainer (without warning).

Due to the fact that our eye must see what's happening, send that signal to the brain, which must in turn relay the message to the index finger and thumb; this is nearly an impossibility!

Let others try it on a partner at their tables.

It wonderfully illustrates the nature of "reaction time" and what often must happen for an employee to react to a customer's need or a company to react to changes in the marketplace.

HANDOUT PICKUP

Although the handout is right in front of him, the volunteer can't get it! The feeling of helplessness is often a good feeling to experience.

Such feelings of helplessness are often at the root of teachability!

Have participants stand in a line against a wall with their heels firmly planted against that wall. Place the handouts in front of them on the floor (about 12" from the wall). A prize awaits the first person who *without bending their knees* can bend over at the waist, pick up the handout, and return to a full standing position without falling away from the wall.

Your prize is safe!

MYSTERY ASHES

Baring his forearm, the trainer shows that it's clean. Yet when the handout is burned and the ashes applied to the arm, a word summarizing the lesson slowly begins to materialize right on his skin! It's weird and memorable!

Although it's a little messy, it's a great closing!

Prior to the training, largely print a summarizing word (i.e., Quality, Team, etc.) on the inside of your forearm with a tube of unflavored original Chapstick! Don't use the cherry flavored or it will show.

When you get ready to close, roll back your sleeve and casually show it to your participants. Burn one of the handouts in a ceremonial fashion — taking some of the resultant ashes and lightly rubbing them on your arm over the prepared area.

You will find the ashes sticking to the Chapstick in a weird fashion until soon everyone in the room can see the word!

Have a towel handy, rub the ashes (and the Chapstick) off and you're ready to take your bow!

THE CANDLE/PART 1

Anyone can blow out a candle! Sure! It's easy! However, no one will believe how difficult it is when blowing through a funnel-shaped handout! Everything is difficult with the wrong tool!

Have a candle burning on your table and challenge someone to blow out the candle — blowing through one of your handouts rolled up into a funnel shape. The person must blow through the small end of the funnel out the large opening of the funnel.

This dissipates the energy of the breath and makes it nearly impossible.

Sometimes it can be done if the very edge of the large opening is held next to the candle flame.

However, applications are always forthcoming as participants see in a graphic manner how difficult even the simplest task can be when trying to do it with the wrong tool.

THE CANDLE/PART 2

Now nonchalantly pick up the candle you just used in the previous demonstration and eat it! Your participants will definitely sit up and pay attention after that!

All you've done is carefully carved a rounded birthday candle shape from an apple and used a sliver from the white meat of a pecan as the wick.

It will light (due to the oil in the pecan), and after you blow it out and wait for the pecan to cool slightly, you can indeed nonchalantly pop the candle in your mouth and eat it!

STICK PUSH

As the handout lays on the floor, three participants attempt to push the broomstick down onto it. With one hand behind his/her back, the trainer successfully resists their attempts. It's a wonderful example of working smarter not harder!

Have your participants hold the broom with the straws pointing toward the ceiling and their hands stacked (see illustration) for about one third the length of the broom. Lay the handout on the floor with the end of the broom handle about eighteen inches above the handout.

Kneel beside the handout and dramatically place one hand behind your back. Place the open palm of your other hand as close to the tip of the broom as possible. Have the rest of your participants make a human circle around this demonstration so that all can see.

Instruct your participant-volunteers that they are to push down on the count of three — attempting to touch the tip of the broom to the handout.

Count to three and then push sideways on the tip of the broom with the palm of your hand — keeping it outside the perimeter of the handout! You're working smarter!

TEARING UP

Can you believe that tearing a handout into three pieces could be so difficult! But it is!

Take a handout and turn it on its side — tearing it as in the diagram.

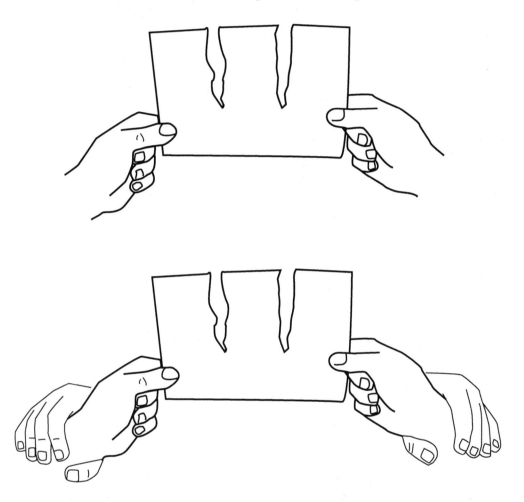

The challenge is for anyone to come to the front of the room, grab the two outside pieces and move their hands apart with such precision that both end pieces tear at the same time and the center piece flutters to the floor.

Anyone who tries it will find it to be impossible to accomplish.

Have someone else volunteer to come to front, stand in front of you (as you turn to the side), grab your wrists as you take hold of the handout ready to show the group how to accomplish this feat. On the count of three, the volunteer should close their eyes (but retain hold of your wrists). Anyone in the audience who doesn't want to see how it's done could also close their eyes at this time.

When you count three, lower your head and grasp the center piece between your lips. Quickly pull your hands apart as you release the center piece so that when the volunteer opens their eyes, they see your hands separated successfully with the center piece on the ground!

A little creativity goes a long way. No one said you couldn't touch the center piece! We must not make up rules that don't exist!

TUBULAR

Take a few moments before the session and you can turn any handout into a magician's production tube. Roll the handout into a tube and produce dollar bills (or other content-related items) as though by magic!

Secretly prepare your copy of the handout ahead of time by folding it in half widthwise with the printing of the handout to the inside of the fold.

Place the folded handout down on your table with the folded edge to the right.

Now make a paper tube out of another handout using scissors and tape. The length of this secret tube should be about 4" to 5" long with a diameter of about 1" to 2".

Use a stapler to staple one end of the tube shut.

Then use your tape to tape the tube onto your folded handout about 1" in from the folded edge and about ½" down from the top. Have the open end of your secret tube at the top.

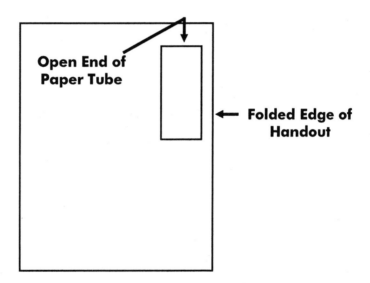

Start rolling your handout from the right edge — wrapping the paper *around* the paper tube. You can then secure this tube with a rubberband. Now you can secretly load the tube with any conten- related item you'd like to produce.

When ready to do a little magic for your participants, pick up the rolled handout being sure to keep the opening of the secret tube to the top and turned slightly away from your participants so that they can't see into the tube. Remove the rubberband and carefully unroll the tube, being sure to keep the secret tube always on the backside, out of the participant's view.

You can now open out the handout fully to presumably show it empty. Of course you can't show both sides of this opened handout. Two or three practices will give you the knack of this unrolling process.

Fold the handout in half again and roll it back into a tube — replacing the rubberband.

You're now ready to begin your production!

Of course it can also be used as a vanish if that suits your purposes better!

Note: If you think simple magic tricks might be a fun way to add to your training toolbox, you're encouraged to consider this author's two volumes of the *Tricks for Trainers* series or the three-volume videotape series entitled, *Tricks for Trainers* Video Library.

TRAINING TRANSPOSITION

With this variation of an old carnival game, you'll use three pieces of paper as your handout —
teaching your participants how to roll them in such a way that they trade places even when another person's finger is holding them down!

When you're ready to have your participants experience this demonstration, distribute two
blank sheets of paper to each person in addition to their handout. The blank pieces should be
the same size as the handout. Explain that you're about to show them a variation of an old carnival game.

Have everyone sandwich their handout between the two pieces of blank paper and begin rolling
the three pieces of paper from the bottom end of the three-paper pile. If they keep rolling the
papers after they get to the end, they will find that the top edges of the papers come around the
tube and fall down onto the table again.

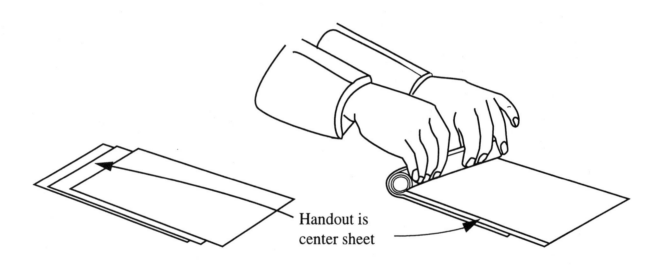

Handout is
center sheet

In the carnival game, the game operator would invite the person to bet as to where the handout
piece is. Is it in the middle? Is it on top? Or is it on the bottom? The operator knew that if he or
she let one only one of the top edges come around the tube and fall to the table before unrolling the tube, the middle piece (the handout) would now be on the bottom. If the operator let
two of the top edges come around the tube and fall to the table before unrolling the tube, the
handout would be on top. And if he or she let none or all of the top three edges come around
the tube and fall to the table before unrolling the tube, the handout would remain in the middle of the stack. The operator used this knowledge to always win when customers would bet
where the handout piece would be. After letting the appropriate number of edges fall, the operator would sometimes use a very nice touch by letting the customer place their finger on the
top edges (thus supposedly precluding any trickery on the part of the operator) before unrolling the tube.

In spite of the fact that its history has this little game making people lose, we can also make it so
that no one ever loses. With this as a goal, it becomes a wonderful illustration of customer service. No customer should ever lose!

Have them try this with a partner. The partner picks where they want the handout to end up (top, middle, bottom) and the operator/participant rolls the paper accordingly so that the partner always wins! That's how good customer service works — always flexing to the demands of the consumer!

THE HANDOUT BOOMERANG

The trainer promises to throw the session handout as hard as possible. She promises that the handout will stop in mid-air (without hitting anything or anyone) and return to her hand! And it does!

This is best done outside or in a room with a very high ceiling. After giving your group a chance to brainstorm about how you're going to turn your handout into a paper boomerang, wad your handout into a ball and throw it as hard as you can straight up in the air. It will do exactly as you promised!

We over complicate so much of life!

SAMSON

Use some of this special paper to make a duplicate handout and have some fun!

Ask your local paper supplier to provide some sample sheets of white TYVEK™ in its heaviest weight. This paper looks and feels quite normal but is untearable!

Some suggestions for its use include:

1) Use white handouts and print one on TYVEK™. Ask for a volunteer to come to the front and demonstrate the power of group suggestibility. Hand him/her a regular handout and have the group repeatedly chant, "You can do it!" Then have the volunteer successfully tear the handout in half.

   Ask the group to repeatedly chant, "You can't do it!" Suddenly, hand the volunteer you're secretly prepared TYVEK™ handout and they will find themselves struggling to tear it. The other participants will love it! Thank the volunteer for the demonstration, have him or her return to his or her seat to a round of applause, and put the prepared handout away so that it can't be examined. I wouldn't tell them how this one was done!

2) You can use a little piece of TYVEK™ in the manner above and simply appear to tear the piece off of one of the handouts — handing it to your volunteer to tear.

PAPER BRIDGE

Can you form your handout into a bridge between two glasses so that it can support a third glass of water? This energizer gets everyone involved!

Make sure that each table has three glasses and some water to work with in this challenge.

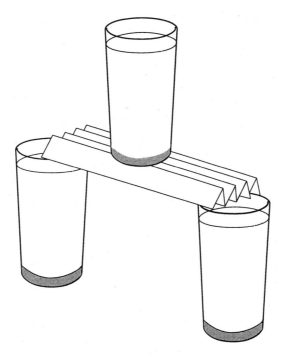

If they accordion pleat the length of their handout with very tight pleats, they will be amazed at the weight that handout will support when placed as a bridge between two glasses!

Try it!

RAINDROPS

The ear is fooled as an imaginary ceiling leak begins to produce audible sounds of dripping right onto the handout! The power of suggestion is very powerful!

Hold a wooden pencil extending out from between your thumb and the middle joint of your index finger (your hand is in a fist). The pencil should be held parallel to the floor.

Place the narrowest edge of your unfolded handout on top of the pencil held in place with your thumb. Have a slight trough down the middle of the paper so that the paper remains rigid as it extends out from the hand.

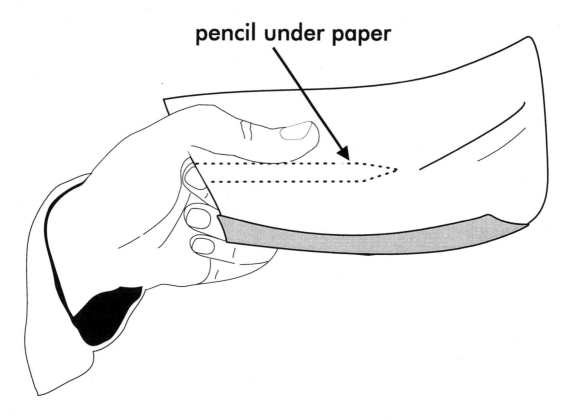

pencil under paper

Now talk about the power of suggestion and point to a place in the training room ceiling where you notice an imaginary leak. Talk about the water dripping onto the carpet and follow the imaginary drips with your eyes.

Extend the paper and pencil into the path of the imaginary drip and slowly push the piece of paper away from you with your thumb. Ask your participants to be sure to tell you when any one of them begins to hear the drops hitting the paper. Keep following the drips with your eyes. By pushing down and away with your thumb on the paper, your participants will soon hear what sounds like drips hitting the paper!

It's quite startling and dramatically underscores how suggestible we really are.

TelePathetic

After anyone writes on a handout, the trainer is able to tell exactly what's on it!

Suddenly ask one of your participants to stand and secretly write any word on the back of his handout. He can show it to the rest of the group if he desires. You'll turn your back so you can't possibly see.

Ask him to fold the paper as small as it can be, and as an extra precaution, request that he place the folded piece of paper under his shoe.

Now you promise that after some concentrating, you will be able to tell him exactly what's on that piece of paper.

You concentrate and concentrate, entering a semi-trance-like state and then dramatically reveal that his foot is on the paper!

Groans will greet you. However, it's a wonderful illustration of how when our communications meet with our listener's assumptions, confusion can often be the result. Finally tell him "exactly what was on the paper!"

ORIGAMIED

There's a prize waiting for anyone who can fold the handout in half and then in half again more than seven times! No one will be able (no matter what size the paper might be), but the group will be energized trying!

It doesn't matter if they use their handout or a piece of flip chart paper, no mere mortal can fold any size piece of paper in half and then in half again more than seven times!

There are some things in life that appear easy but aren't!

SPEEDY SCISSORS SNIP!

With quite a flair, the trainer tosses the handout into the air and apparently uses his scissors to snip a piece off the handout in mid-air! It's showy! It's easy! Everyone enjoys learning it!

Prior to the arrival of your participants, cut a sliver of paper from your handout and secretly place it *between* the closed blades of a pair of scissors.

When you're ready to begin, indicate to your group that you've been practicing a feat that's really quite sensational.

As the participants drum on the table, hold your closed scissors in one hand and the handout paper in the other. Raise the paper high into the air and release it so that it flutters toward the ground. Stab your scissors towards the paper and snip at the paper. The piece of paper will fall from between the blades, but it will look as though you snipped a piece of paper in mid-air!

After you show them how you did it, your group will understand that many things look difficult but really aren't!

FINGERTIP BALANCING

With a drum roll from the group, the trainer balances the entire handout from just one corner on his fingertip! Everyone wants to try once they see how it's done!

Take your handout and put a *gentle* crease in the paper between two diagonal corners. Extend your index finger and balance one of those diagonal corners on the tip of that finger. Gently keep your arm moving back and forth to get all the help you can from the air currents, and you will be as amazed as your participants that you can keep it balanced there!

This dramatic demonstration can even be done with a tabloid size page of newspaper!

It shows how impossible-sounding feats can really be easy with a little training!

PAPER DOLLS

With a few snips of the scissors, the trainer folds the handout and cuts out a perfect line of content icons (a.k.a. paper dolls) as a wonderful way to close the training session!

Secretly take one of your handouts and make a paper string of content icons (i.e., customers, computer disks, question marks, exclamation points, smiley faces, etc.).

Take care in making this set and you'll be able to use it over and over again.

Cut out the icons and accordion pleat them into a small packet. Then use a glue stick to glue one side of the folded packet to the backside of another handout.

At the conclusion of your training, show and fold the secretly prepared handout (with apparently very precise folds being careful not to show your participants the backside and the prepared icon string) and begin cutting the handout with a pair of scissors. All you're going to do is to cut away all the paper *except* the string of icons glued to the back. However, make it look more difficult than that!

When the paper has been cut away from around the prepared string of icons, pull your hands apart and display your handiwork!

Your participants will give you much credit for your cleverness and skill!

And if I were you, I'd let them believe what they wanted and keep the secret to myself!

FOOT LIFT

Standing with his or her right foot against the wall, a volunteer attempts to lift his or her left foot into the air balancing the handout on the top of his or her shoe! The difficulty is hilarious! Finally, the trainer shows that it can be done!

Here is how the challenge unfolds! Ask a volunteer to stand with the right side of his or her right foot flush against the wall's baseboard. The handout is gingerly placed on top of the left shoe. The goal is to lift the left foot up in the air without dropping the handout off the shoe. Give it a try! It's impossible!

However, offer to show how with many years of practice you've accomplished the task.

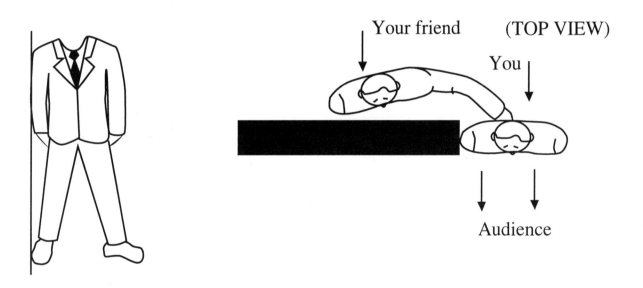

Stand in a doorway of the room and put your right foot flush against the door jamb. Unbeknownst to the participants, you've enlisted the help of a friend to secretly be on the other side of the wall ready to reach out and grab your belt — pulling you even tighter against the jamb of the door.

You will then be able to lift your left foot slowly into the air and even wave it around a little without spilling the handout or falling over yourself!

After lowering your foot back to the ground, your secret assistant slips away, and you'll find others are now inspired to keep trying this impossible task! Or, you can introduce your secret assistant and show how the impossible can be made possible with teamwork.

THROUGH THE EYE OF A NEEDLE

Pin one of these impossibilities to each handout and listen to the discussion begin! This sewing needle has at least twenty-seven threads through the single eye! How is it even possible? The trainer isn't telling!

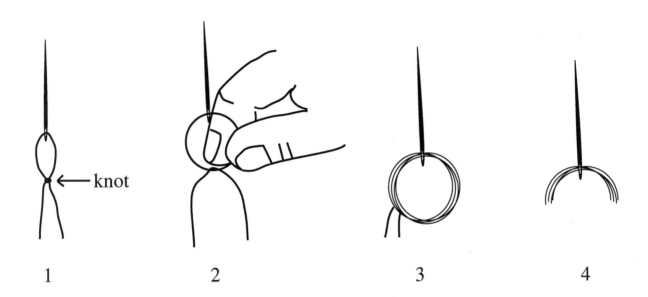

1   2   3   4

To prepare this unusual exhibit, thread a sewing needle with a one-yard length of thread. The larger the eye of the needle, the easier the following task. Pull the thread through until the two ends are even and the needle is in the middle of the thread. The needle is held by its point with its eye closest to the floor.

Then tie the right side of the thread around the left side of the thread (use a double knot) at a point about four inches below the needle's eye (Diagram #2). If you pull on the right side of the thread at a point above the knot, you will find the thread pulled up and through the eye of needle many, many times with each pull. Eventually the entire eye of the needle will be packed full with thread. Then simply cut the threads as shown in Diagram #4 so that the result will be a needle with many, many threads through a single eye.

It does, indeed, look like an impossibility and is a great way to illustrate how impossible-appearing feats can be accomplished with a carefully planned strategy!

Zip I & II!

Can you remove the handout so that the stack of quarters remain on the opening of the ketchup bottle? Remember hearing about the tablecloth and dishes trick? Give it a try! Then increase the difficulty and try to think of an entirely new way!

Set a capped glass ketchup bottle on the table and place your handout on top of the bottle held with a stack of about ten or twelve quarters. Only about ½" of your handout is inserted under the stack.

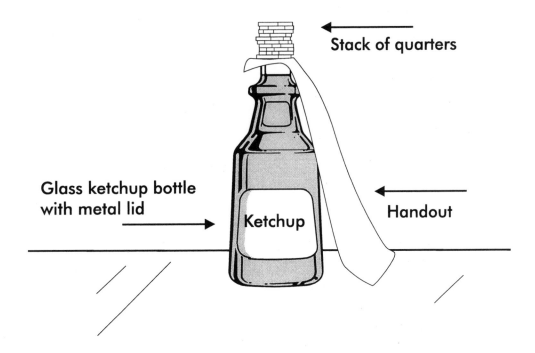

The challenge to your participants is to remove the handout without spilling the quarters. You may not touch the quarters with anything!

After giving them time to brainstorm, show them how by quickly pulling *down* on the trapped handout close to the point where it rests under the quarters, the handout will slip out from underneath the quarters just like that famous demonstration of the tablecloth removal with a full table of dishes. The inertia of the quarters works in your favor!

However, now set up yet another challenge! Put the handout over the top of the ketchup bottle with half of the handout going down each side of the bottle. Then stack the quarters on top of the handout and pleat the handout several times on each side of the stack of quarters to eliminate the possibility of being able to pull it, as in the previous demonstration, without spilling the quarters.

The challenge is the same. The handout must be removed without spilling the quarters. Again, you are not allowed to touch the quarters with your hand or anything else.

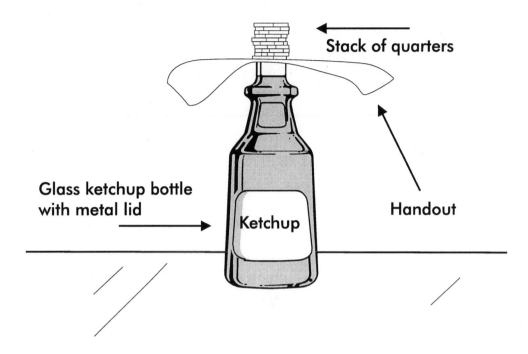

In this challenge their previous experience with these same props will actually make solving this one more difficult!

However, if you slowly tear the handout in from both sides until only a little untorn piece holds the handout together underneath the pile of quarters, you'll be able to pull quickly down on the handout from both sides. The handout will tear and pull out from underneath the stack of quarter without spilling one of them!

The handout will be destroyed, but that was never a rule!

THE THORNLESS ROSE

With a wonderful story about a rose and the power of one person being willing to change, the trainer summarizes the training session in a very powerful manner while slowly transforming his or her own handout into an intriguing paper rose.

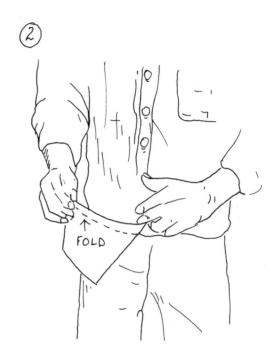

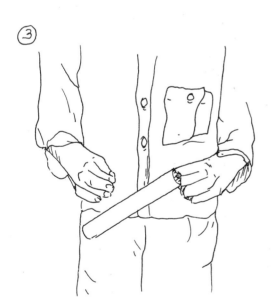

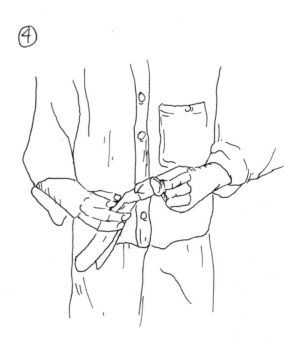

Learning to make the paper rose is the first step toward mastering this powerful presentation piece.

1) Hold a handout in reading position so that you are looking at its printed side. However, hold the handout upside down. While holding it in this position, fold about two inches of the top of the handout away from you and crease this fold. The reason the handout was initially turned upside down was so that this folded piece would probably not have any printing on it.

2) Hold the top edge at one corner between your index and middle finger and begin rolling the paper around those two fingers so that the folded edge of the paper is being rolled to the outside and the printed side is being rolled to the inside (see diagram).

3) After rolling the entire handout into a tube, tightly pinch together the handout from the outside at the very tips of your index and middle finger and gently remove those two fingers from inside what will be the blossom of the flower.

4) Now tightly twist the handout for about half its length beginning at the base of the flower's blossom. When you reach the halfway point, reach down and grab the exposed corner at the bottom of the handout and bring it up to about the halfway point in the stem of the flower to form the leaf. It will need to be pulled out and shaped to look like a leaf with the remainder of the stem tightly twisted below the leaf down to the end of the stem.

5) As a final touch, shape the blossom and fold up with a crease the exposed corner on the outside of the blossom to give it even more the appearance of a rose.

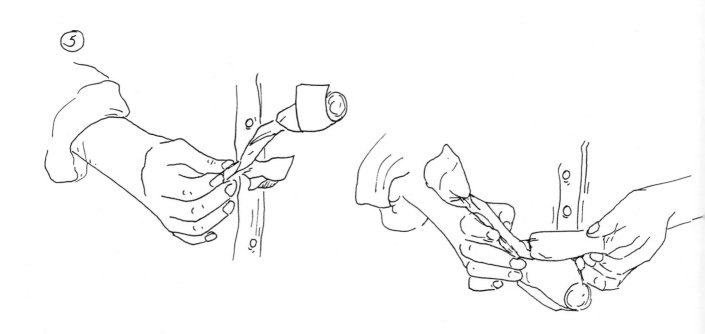

The story you tell is this…

"There once was a man who brought a rose into his home. It was just a single rose, but he found a jar, used it as a vase and set it in his dining room. The next day when he got up, he looked at the beautiful rose in that vase and suddenly noticed that the walls of the dining room looked dingy and dirty in comparison. So he decided to paint the walls of that room.

The very next day, he admired his rose and the freshly painted walls of his dining room and realized that the adjoining living room looked dingy compared to the dining room. So he gave the living room a fresh coat of paint that very day.

However, he soon realized that now the carpeting and the rest of the house needed paint too because in comparison to the living room and the dining room, the rest of the house looked so dark and dirty.

He did replace the carpeting and paint the rest of the house until that single rose had spread its influence throughout the entire house. That's the power of a single rose or a single person willing to influence the world around them with their own form of beauty and strength. May you be a rose!"

And may these handout ideas help you be a rose in the lives of your participants!

ADDENDUM

BIOGRAPHY OF THE AUTHOR

DAVE ARCH

Best-selling author, Creative Training Techniques Senior Trainer, professional magician, and trainer-of-trainers, Dave Arch has authored *Tricks for Trainers, Volumes I & II, The Tricks For Trainers Video Library* (three volumes), *First Impressions/Lasting Impressions, Showmanship For Presenters,* and this, his newest release, *Red Hot Handouts.* His accomplishments in the training field are honored in the *1996-97 National Directory of Who's Who in Executives and Professionals.*

As a Senior Trainer for Bob Pike's Creative Training Techniques International, Inc. Dave Arch presents the seminars, *Techniques and Tricks* and *Showmanship For Presenters.* In a two-day session he leads trainers through an experience of 119 attention management techniques as found in his books.

Dave has literally pioneered the use of magic in training. Since 1982, magic has proven itself an effective communication tool for groups as diverse as hospital CEOs to sales representatives to banking administrators.

Combining a ten-year background in personal and family counseling with a professional expertise in magic, Dave travels from his home in Omaha, Nebraska, to present his unique presentations before some 25,000 people each year in both corporate and conference settings.

ROBERT W. PIKE, C.S.P.

Bob Pike has developed and implemented training programs for business, industry, government and the professions since 1969. As president of Creative Training Techniques International, Inc., and publisher of Creative Training Techniques Press, Bob leads sessions over 150 days per year covering topics of leadership, attitudes, motivation, communication, decision-making, problem-solving, personal and organizational effectiveness, conflict management, team building and managerial productivity. More than 60,000 trainers have attended the Creative Training Techniques™ workshop. As a consultant, Bob has worked with such organizations as Pfizer, UpJohn, Caesar Boardwalk Regency, Exhibitor Magazine, Hallmark Cards and IBM.

Over the years Bob has contributed to magazines such as *Training, The Personal Administrator* and *The Self-Development Journal*. He is editor of the *Creative Training Techniques Newsletter* and is author of *The Creative Training Techniques Handbook,* and *Improving Managerial Productivity.*

WIN *Rave Reviews*
on your next **Presentation**

"I have never felt so enthusiastic about a program! This workshop is a MUST for any trainer, regardless of level of experience."

Susan Russell, Bank One

Do you talk so people really listen?

Bob Pike's Creative Training Techniques™ Seminar

Find out why over 65,000 trainers love Creative Training Techniques. What makes this seminar so different? You'll learn how to get your participants enthusiastically involved in the training. By creating an interactive learning environment, you'll watch the attendees excitement go up and up and up. The result? Your group will easily learn twice as much. When they apply their new skills on the job, you'll see dramatic results.

Learn a revolutionary training approach—Participant-Centered Training. This teaching style is far more effective than traditional lecture-based training. Over 65,000 trainers world-wide have attended this seminar and applied these participant-centered training techniques to their work environments. More effective training means a more valuable and effective work force. Register today so you can get rave reviews on your next presentation. Over 140 public seminars are scheduled in 40 different cities each year.

In-house Training Seminars

Customized programs for trainers, sales staff, and technical presenters developed for 100s of organizations. Give us a call so we can discuss how to help your company increase work force performance by maximizing the impact of your training. Just a few of our clients who have brought Creative Training Techniques programs in-house:

American Express • AT&T • GE Plastics • State Farm Insurance • 3M • Tonka Corporation

Creative Solutions Catalog

Insider's Tips to Double the Impact of Your Presentation

Filled with fun, stimulating, creative resources including games, magic, music, wuzzles, books, tapes, videos, software, presentation graphics—everything you need to make your presentation an absolute winner.

Creative Training Techniques
International, Inc.

1-800-383-9210
www.cttbobpike.com

Creative Training Techniques International, Inc. • 7620 W. 78th Street, Mpls. MN 55439 • (612) 829-1954 • Fax (612) 829-0260

Bob Pike's
Creative Training Techniques™
Train-the-Trainer Conference

*The only conference dedicated exclusively
to the participant-centered approach to training*

- Learn about the revolutionary, participant-centered training approach—the breakthrough alternative to lecture-based training
- See the nation's leading training consultants model their very best participant-centered activities
- Experience the power of participant-centered techniques to dramatically increase retention
- Learn about innovative training transfer techniques adopted by leading Fortune 500 companies
- Discover powerful management strategies that clearly demonstrate the business results for your training programs

Just a few of the companies who have sent groups (not just individuals) to the Conference

**American Express • AT&T • Caterpillar • First Bank
Southern Nuclear Operating Company • State Farm • United HealthCare • US West**

Rave Reviews!

"I refer to my conference workbook all the time. I've shared the techniques with my trainers, and my own evaluations have improved. Our needs analysis now produces actionable input. My comfort level with our line managers has increased—at my first meeting with them where I used what I learned at the conference, they applauded. Now that's positive feedback!"

Gretchen Gospodarek, Training Manager, **TCF Bank Wisconsin**

"For any trainer who wants to move beyond lecture-based training, I recommend Bob Pike's participant-centered seminars and in-house consultants."

Ken Blanchard, Co-Author of *The One-Minute Manager*

"Bob Pike is creating a new standard in the industry by which all other programs will soon be measured."

Elliott Masie, President, **The MASIE Center**

Visit our Web site: www.cttbobpike.com to learn more about the Conference, Creative Training Techniques International, Inc. or the Participant-Centered Training approach.

1-800-383-9210
www.cttbobpike.com

Creative Training Techniques International, Inc. • 7620 W. 78th St., Mpls., MN 55439 • 612-829-1954 • Fax 612-829-0260

13 Questions to Ask *Before* You Bring Anyone In-House

An in-house program is an investment. You want to ensure high return. Here are 13 questions to ask before you ask anyone to train your trainers (or train anyone else!).

1. What kind of measurable results have other clients had from your training?
2. How much experience does this company have in training trainers?
3. Is this 100 percent of what the company does or just part of what it does?
4. How experienced are the trainers who will work with our people?
5. How experienced are your trainers in maximizing training transfer to the job?
6. Is the program tailored to my needs, or is it the same content as the public program?
7. Why is an in-house program to our advantage?
8. Is team-building a by-product of the seminar?
9. Is there immediate application of new skills during the training session?
10. What kinds of resource and reference materials do we get?
11. What type of pre-course preparation or post-course follow-up do you do?
12. How are our participants recognized for their achievements?
13. Will you teach my trainers how to get participant buy-in, even from the difficult participant?

Advantages of a Customized, In-House Program with Creative Training Techniques™ International, Inc.

Customized in-house programs provide your organization with training tailored to your specific needs. Our unique participant-centered teaching style is a revolutionary new training approach that is far more effective than traditional lecture-based training. This training approach has been adapted by a wide range of industries including healthcare, finance, communications, government, and non-profit agencies. Our clients include American Express, AT&T, Hewlett-Packard, 3M, U.S. Healthcare, and Tonka Corporation. We are eager to learn about your training needs and discuss how we can provide solutions. Please give us a call so we can help your company create a more vital and effective workforce.

 Creative Training Techniques
International, Inc.

1–800–383–9210
www.cttbobpike.com

Creative Training Techniques International, Inc. • 7620 W. 78th St., Mpls., MN 55439 • 612-829-1954 • Fax 612-829-0260

More great resources from Jossey-Bass/Pfeiffer!

End your sessions with a BANG!

Lynn Solem
& Bob Pike

50 Creative Training Closers

They'll forget you as soon as you walk out the door—unless you make your training memorable. This essential resource is your way to make your mark. Fifty ways to close your training sessions and presentations so they won't forget you—or your training.

Many trainers start training sessions memorably with a rousing icebreaker, or with a spirited overview of what's to follow. But you're probably letting the ends slip through your fingers. Some trainers conclude training sessions by looking at their watches and saying, "Oh, time's up! Goodbye!" By trailing off with a whisper, you're missing an opportunity to reinforce your training. You're helping your participants to forget everything you've taught them. Stop this brain drain by ending with a bang! This invaluable book is packed with practical closers.

You get activities great for:
- *Reviewing* material
- *Celebrating* success
- *Motivating* participants . . . and more!

Solem and Pike show you all the essentials, and preparation is quick and easy. So little time to invest for such a HUGE payoff! This book is training dynamite—make it your secret weapon today.

paperback / 96 pages
....
50 Creative Training Closers
Item #F439

Bob Pike &
Dave Arch

Dealing with Difficult Participants

127 Practical Strategies for Minimizing Resistance and Maximizing Results in Your Presentations

Everyone knows them . . . but almost no one knows how to deal with them. Difficult participants. The "latecomer." The "know-it-all." The "confused." What do you do? Train-the-trainer master Bob Pike and magician/trainer Dave Arch have the answers.

Learn to deal with types such as:
- The Preoccupied
- The Socializer
- The Introvert
- The Bored
- The Domineering
- The Unqualified
- The Skeptic
- The Sleeper . . . and others!

Don't let difficult participants get the best of you. You can't afford not to pick up this engaging book. Maximize the learning potential in all your presentations with *Dealing With Difficult Participants*!

paperback / 150 pages
....
Dealing with Difficult Participants
Item #F244

To order, please contact your local bookstore, call us toll-free at 1-800-274-4434, or visit us on the Web at www.pfeiffer.com.